Additional Praise for *Radical Awareness*

"Catherine Dowling has much to offer: eloquence, insight, and profound wisdom about living life abundantly … [This book offers] a series of practices that will help readers experience that same abundance on a daily basis."

—Kelsea Habecker, author of *Hollow Out*

"*Radical Awareness* is a compelling read. The combination of wisdom, spiritual awareness, and poetic writing engaged me."

—Charlotte Robin Cook, former publisher and
acquisition editor for KOMENAR Publishing

"This book gives us a tool kit for opening our minds, our eyes, and our hearts to the infinite possibilities life offers."

—Joy Manné, PhD, author of *Conscious Breathing in Everyday Life*

RADICAL
AWARENESS

ABOUT THE AUTHOR

Catherine Dowling is one of the leading writers in the field of breathwork psychotherapy. Her book *Rebirthing and Breathwork: A Powerful Technique for Personal Transformation* is essential reading for students of breathwork therapy and has attracted thousands of readers to breathwork as their path of spiritual and psychological development.

Catherine is a former president of the International Breathwork Foundation in addition to being a founder and former chairperson of the Irish Rebirthing Psychotherapy Association and co-founder of the Federation of Irish Complementary Therapy Associations.

As the author of influential articles on the training of therapists, Catherine has worked on the development of training standards for breathwork organizations in the US and England. She developed the nationally accredited Rebirther Training Program for the training of therapists in Ireland and was a member of the Irish Department of Health's national working group on the regulation of complementary and alternative therapists. She was also a consultant evaluator to the Irish Health Services Executive on the issues of suicide prevention and residential child care.

RADICAL
AWARENESS

5
PRACTICES
FOR A
FULLY ENGAGED
LIFE

CATHERINE
DOWLING

Llewellyn Publications
Woodbury, Minnesota

FIRST EDITION
First Printing, 2014

Cover art: www.iStockphoto.com/9712604/© IakovKalinin
Cover design by Lisa Novak
Editing by Andrea Neff
Interior art by the Llewellyn Art Department

Llewellyn Publishing is a registered trademark of Llewellyn Worldwide Ltd.

Library of Congress Cataloging-in-Publication Data
Dowling, Catherine, 1956–
    Radical awareness : 5 practices for a fully engaged life / by Catherine Dowling. — First edition.
        pages cm
    Includes bibliographical references.
    ISBN 978-0-7387-4014-0
    1. Spiritual life. 2. Conduct of life. 3. Self-realization. 4. Breathing exercises. I. Title.
    BL624.D686 2014
    158—dc23
                        2014031847

Llewellyn Publications
A Division of Llewellyn Worldwide Ltd.
2143 Wooddale Drive
Woodbury, MN 55125-2989
www.llewellyn.com

Printed in the United States of America

OTHER BOOKS BY CATHERINE DOWLING

Rebirthing and Breathwork:
A Powerful Technique for Personal Transformation
(Piatkus Books, 2000)

The only boundaries to our horizons are those we draw ourselves…
We half-heartedly and piously settle for less.
There is no "fire in our bellies" to make us shout at God.
Instead of storming heaven like privileged warrior-children…,
we hang around behind the shadows,
wondering if the Lord of the castle is in a good mood.
~DANIEL O'LEARY, *TRAVELLING LIGHT*

To
John and Mary Dowling
for gifts beyond count, including the love of books

Contents

EXERCISES

INTRODUCTION

Damian's life changed forever one spring morning in the middle of a country lane.

Two years earlier, his wife of thirty years had left him. Over the years, people had come and gone from his life, jobs had lasted a while and then ended, friends' marriages seemed happy and then dissolved. But Damian's marriage endured. In a world of constant change, the relationship with his wife was the one fixed point he could depend on. Then it, too, ended—and with it went everything that was solid and sure in his world. Damian floundered, scrambling for anything that was certain, anything he could trust to last, to be what it appeared to be.

In the early months of his divorce, medication gave him relief from the pain. A therapist recommended by his doctor helped him tame the anger and anguish that threatened to tear him apart. But two years on, Damian's mind still raced incessantly, screaming for ... he didn't know what for. He told friends he wanted a cliff to jump off of. He didn't mean it literally—he wasn't suicidal—but it was the only image he could come up with to describe the incredible frustration he felt with his life.

His therapist suggested meditation, and so he had spent the previous six Saturday mornings in a wellness center struggling to master a range of meditation techniques. Six wasted Saturdays, in his opinion. The meditation teacher talked about letting go of mind. Damian couldn't understand the concept and he couldn't get past it, no matter what technique they used.

That weekend the topic was walking meditation. After instruction and practice, the teacher told the class to go outside and find a place to walk alone. Damian chose an overgrown lane that ran past the back of the wellness center. He followed the instructions carefully—walk slowly, feel every step, notice whatever came to his attention but don't think about it, just notice it. As he walked, he felt every tiny movement of sinew and bone. That was new. He'd never been aware of his body like that before. Then he noticed the grass, each silvery blade moving independently, glinting in the pale morning sunlight. Primroses studded the grassy banks of the lane. Their delicate yellow petals seemed more vivid than usual, their leaves a deeper, more textured green.

"They're incredible," he thought, then grappled with the instruction not to think.

On the path ahead of him lay a small leaf glistening with moisture from an earlier rain shower. Damian picked it up. The leaf rested lightly in the palm of his hand while he stared at the exquisite lacework of veins magnified by the crystal mound of a raindrop. He felt an overwhelming tide of love well up inside him.

He looked up at the tree the leaf had fallen from. Its limbs stretched into the sky, green with young leaves. Damian felt himself merge with the tree. The sky beyond its branches washed over him, through him, saturated him. He loved the sky, the tree, the leaf. He trusted them, became one with them. They cradled him in a world without past or future, in a single, sure point of absolute stillness.

What Is Oneness?

What happened to Damian that Saturday illustrates some of the classic elements of a mystical spiritual experience of union, or *oneness*: the expansion of awareness so that he noticed every detail of what was happening inside him as it happened; the falling away of conditioning and limitations (in Damian's case, his need for surety in life); expansion into nature; pure, immediate, raw, direct experience of the moment. All of this led to a feeling of intense aliveness, freedom, and love. But the key element was the experience of oneness with everything, with the sky, the tree, the leaf, life itself.

Damian's spiritual experience in the lane goes by many names. Psychologist Abraham Maslow coined the term "peak state" to describe it. Ancient religious traditions use the word "mysticism." Others call it expanded awareness, altered consciousness, a trip. And a 2002 Gallop Poll showed that 41 percent of Americans (around 80 million adults) had experienced just such a profound "experience or awakening that changed the direction of [their] life."[1]

My first mystical experience occurred when I was still in my teens. Over subsequent years, oneness states occurred spontaneously from time to time, as they do for many people. I just accepted them as something that happens. But when I began to train as a breathwork therapist, I discovered that mystical experiences often occur during breathwork sessions, particularly toward the end of a session. When I established my breathwork therapy practice, I watched the same thing happen for my clients. Now, after seventeen years as a breathwork therapist, I've had the privilege of being present to hundreds of clients as they entered mystical states, both in one-to-one and in group breathwork sessions. My personal and professional experience confirms that these mystical states, portals to the spiritual life, are ours for the taking, freely available through something as simple and routine as breathing.

Oneness states are not figments of an overactive imagination. They're not questionable psychological episodes best kept to yourself. These states arise spontaneously, and for those who meditate consistently or engage in other spiritually nurturing activities, they can be a regular experience. In other words, they're natural occurrences.

In terms of design, nature is lean. It rarely produces anything superfluous, so if something exists, it has a role to play. The intensity of mystical states fades, sometimes quickly, sometimes gradually. But these wonderful experiences contain within them all the information we need to help us live a full, vibrant life, every day of our lives. The experience of oneness is our guide, our mentor, in the great adventure of living our lives as fully and freely as we possibly can. This is what Damian discovered when he took his walk in the lane.

ONENESS AND TRANSFORMATION

Damian's mystical experience faded over the next few days, but he had been changed by it. He had learned to trust, not people, not permanence, but life itself. He chose to explore and solidified his newly won trust through a series of breathwork sessions. In those sessions he learned the skills mystical spiritual experiences teach us, the skills we will explore in detail in this book: self-awareness, how to live in the present moment, how to live with the discomfort of letting life happen without a plan to control it. Three months later, he left his once solid, planned life behind and headed off to Rwanda as a volunteer. I never saw Damian again, but he kept in touch. He settled in Rwanda and is now a teacher there. That's not a future he ever envisaged for himself. At times the living is not easy, but he has willingly traded his old life for the exuberance of full-on living that his experience of trust opened up for him.

CHASING HAPPINESS

According to a US Department of Health and Human Services report, in 2011 an estimated 45.6 million Americans had a serious mental health disorder, including depression.[2] Countless others experiences low-level unhappiness—a niggling dissatisfaction with life or some aspect of it that eludes our power to control or change. In our Western world, we're often told we can acquire happiness. So we look outside ourselves to a better job, a better home, a new diet, a fitness program. We strive to make our relationship work better, or to leave a relationship that's not working, to have more friends, to do more things. There is nothing intrinsically wrong with any of this, but as a recipe for happiness, the approach carries a high risk of failure.

Every client I've worked with over the past two decades as a breathwork therapist has come to therapy because they discovered for themselves the fact that we can't become happy from the outside in. It works in reverse. When we change on the inside, when we experience within us the peace, love, and aliveness we crave, then the outside, our life circumstances, begin to change, begin to reflect our inner reality. The problem lies not so much in what we strive for, but in the fact that we are striving at all.

Author and spiritual teacher Richard Rohr is fond of saying that how you get there determines where you arrive. We try to improve the quality of our lives. We add and subtract from it to achieve this. But the real issue is not the type of life we have. It's the manner in which we live it.

FULL ENGAGEMENT LIVING

Living fully is not about acquiring, shedding, or even changing anything in our lives. Living fully is fundamentally a deep, vibrant engagement with the rich texture of every moment. It's about being fully present, fully awake as we go through our days, deeply connected to both ourselves and our surroundings. Living fully brings a joy that transcends our circumstances. It unlocks within us an intense love of life and, at the same time, a sense of being loved and held by that life. It offers us a sense of security that is not dependent on relationships or possessions. Whether we believe in a god or not, we come to know the meaning of the biblical phrase "I have engraved you on the palms of my hands" (Isaiah 49:16).

Embracing life is a spiritual experience, an inner exploration. The outer circumstances of our lives can act as a catalyst and a teacher, but spiritual growth happens when we face inward toward our deepest feelings, when we challenge our most cherished beliefs, and when we recognize the significance of the experiences that have shaped our lives. There may be painful confrontations with ourselves and our past, but ultimately the journey inward leads us into joyful union with nature, with life, and most of all with ourselves.

The spiritual journey is full of paradoxes, as we quickly discover, and one of the greatest is that when we give up striving for change and enter into that union with life, change comes to us unforced. Life will present us with a richness that far exceeds what we dreamed of. That richness may be different from what we thought we wanted, but better than anything we could ever have imagined, because how we get there determines where we arrive. This engagement with life was the metaphorical cliff Damian talked about. Once he jumped off that cliff, once he trusted in a future he could not foresee, a new life opened up for him. That life was richer and more satisfying than anything he could ever have planned.

Our guide to living such a fully engaged life is the wisdom and transformation we gain from our own mystical experiences, from the states of oneness that are available to us through spiritual practices like breathwork, meditation, yoga, or dance, but also through simply being open to our own spiritual nature.

WORKING WITH THIS BOOK

Spirituality is the ground we walk upon, the air we breathe, the life within us, and everything that surrounds us, and one of its most amazing manifestations is the state of oneness. Over thousands of hours facilitating breathwork sessions for clients and hundreds of breathwork sessions in which I was the client, I've tried to work out what exactly the experience of oneness can teach us about how to live well day to day. I've discovered five key aspects of the mystical state of oneness that I call "practices." These practices are approaches to living and life that, if followed, can transform the way we experience our world.

This book is about using these five practices as a guide to personal growth. Oneness experiences change us and the way we view the world, but they also provide us with the recipe for taking charge of our own experience of life and transforming our way of living into something infinitely satisfying and enlivening. Embracing the five practices empowers us to transcend and transform our circumstances. Through them, we find treasure everywhere, even in the grimmest of situations.

In part 1, we will explore a variety of oneness states from the lives of ordinary people. We'll look at how an experience of oneness can change us, almost miraculously, as it did Damian. But more importantly, we will explore what oneness teaches us about how to live our lives day to day through the five practices. The practices provide us with a map for our spiritual, emotional, and psychological growth, a blueprint for full engagement living. This section of the book lays the foundation for putting the practices into action.

In part 2, we will learn how to access oneness and the wisdom it offers through meditation and through the power of our own breath. We will then learn how to apply the five practices to life. It can be difficult to see what prevents us from living fully, from flourishing. Therefore, in this section of the book, each chapter will focus on one of the many ways we hold ourselves back—the attitudes that sabotage our best intentions, the behavior patterns we long to be free of but keep repeating, the situations we see no way out of. Through the five practices, we will bring the wisdom of oneness states to bear on these issues in a practical way.

Parallel to my breathwork therapy practice, I worked extensively as a group facilitator and trainer. In that role, I facilitated groupwork sessions for businesses, state agencies, and community-based nonprofits. I've facilitated personal development programs for women's and men's groups and for teenagers. I've also worked for many years with women caught in abusive relationships. The exercises sprinkled throughout each chapter of this book are the fruit of that experience. They are designed to help you embody the five practices, to turn theory into action and put the practices to work in your own life. By working the practices, we ourselves can be transformed so that if heaven is a fully lived life, we can storm our particular heaven with passion and abandon.

The more we use the five practices, the more we clear out the obstacles we face to living a free, full life. We shed old ways of thinking, old ways of reacting to life that no longer serve us well. Over time, our lives become calmer, more interesting, more engaged. Emotional highs and lows even out and are replaced by an enduring vitality, a vitality that is nourished by a deep connection with ourselves and with life. We know the peace that lies at the heart of stillness and we enjoy the freedom to co-create and shape our own existence. This is where the five practices eventually take us, our ultimate goal. This book is about doing the work, through exercises, breathwork, and meditation, that will put us on the road to that goal.

PART 1
THE FIVE PRACTICES

Endemic to every human heart is a spark of infinity,
a hint of the divine, a small mystic
who has designs on eternity.

~DANIEL O'LEARY

1
WHAT IS ONENESS?

Behind your image, below your words,
above your thoughts, the silence of another world waits.
—JOHN O'DONOHUE, *ANAM CARA*

Beatle John Lennon once asked producer George Martin to make a track they were working on "sound like an orange." We catalogue our world in much the same way that librarians catalogue books. We look for groups and categories, shapes and patterns. Oranges fall within the category of food, subsection fruit. A Beatles song falls within the category of music, subsection rock. The boundaries between two such distinct categories generally don't dissolve—but they did for John Lennon.

Lennon had a particularly creative imagination. He was also steeped in the psychotropic drug culture of the 1960s. LSD, synthesized in 1938 but made famous by the '60s counterculture movement, dissolves perceptual boundaries. The demarcation lines that separate the categories of our mental library fade under its influence. Meditation and other spiritual practices can have a similar effect. John Lennon used LSD and he meditated. He could imagine music sounding like an orange. He may even have experienced music that way too.

Mystical spiritual experiences, regardless of how they come about, often lead to a perception of oneness. In a state of oneness, we unlearn much of what we thought we knew. The forms and shapes of our world—like those of a sound and an orange—become fluid. Things that seemed vitally important and true are no longer relevant. We have opened up a new way of seeing and being. We have opened a portal to our spirituality, and through it we enter a world where even the shapes and forms by which we categorize reality become flexible.

This is a world of inner freedom, of peace and love. Here our connection with our core self and with life is so complete and so intimate, we desire nothing more than to live fully in this present moment.

Oneness experiences can be brief, from a few moments to an hour or less. They can also take an extended form, lasting from days to years. These experiences take many shapes. The Institute for the Study of Peak States has categorized them into fifteen different types, and the institute's founder, Grant McFetridge, identified over forty varieties of these mystical states in various cultures and spiritual traditions.[3] Here are a few more examples.

The Road to Damascus

The most famous oneness experience of all is St. Paul's conversion on the road to Damascus. Paul of Tarsus and a group of colleagues set out on the road to Damascus. Paul carried a letter from the High Priest of the Temple in Jerusalem, giving him the authority to arrest and detain any Christians he met in Damascus. Their aim was to suppress the Christian movement in the city.

Descriptions of what happened along the road vary, but include Paul seeing a bright light and hearing a voice that had a profound and lasting effect on him. Scientists have since argued over precisely what happened to Paul. Some think he had a severe migraine or an epileptic fit. None have agreed on a single "scientific" cause, but all agree on his conversion.

"Conversion" is a religious term that means being turned around. The experience on the Damascus Road turned Paul from a zealous persecutor of Christians into a preacher of Christianity and a leader of the Christian church. He became one with the people he had once tried to annihilate.

Here is a description of an event in the early life of Lisa, one of my clients. Far less dramatic than Paul's conversion, it was nonetheless profound for her. She was sixteen at the time and standing at the back of a high school science class. The experience occurred spontaneously, or at least she couldn't recall anything leading up to it.

"They were doing some experiment with gas burners," she explained. "I hated lighting them. My hand would shake so much I'd drop the match. I hated it. I was looking at all these people that I was afraid of and it was like the light changed or something. Everything got brighter... the colors got more vivid. Then I was free. Just like that, I was free. I was with all these girls I was afraid of most of the time, and all I could feel was that I loved every one of them. They were all so beautiful, as people I mean, and I loved them. I wasn't afraid. It was the first time in my life I wasn't afraid." Lisa suffered from excruciating shyness and had come to accept constant fear as normal in her life, for the rest of her life. At sixteen, she tasted the freedom that came from the love she felt for her classmates. Over the coming years, buoyed by this memory, she worked successfully in therapy to make that freedom from fear a daily reality in her life.

Here is a oneness state initiated by a breathwork practice. It comes from another client, Angela. "I was on a small boat. It was moving forward. It made ripples in the water, but nobody was rowing. There was no engine. I was completely alone. The sky was iridescent blue and white, like luminous plankton. It swirled around me. I could smell food, but there wasn't any, just the smell. I think it was Chinese food. I think I was in China. My hands were very white. Bits of sky moved around me. I could grab hold of it, and then it passed through my hands. Then there was a fountain, only the water wasn't water. It was a fountain of light, shooting up into the sky and cascading down again. It was so beautiful. I had never felt like that before. I had never felt so full I didn't need anything else."

Angela's experience was sensual, visual, a little psychedelic. The poetry of the nineteenth-century British Romantics beautifully expressed this kind of sensory fluidity.[4] During oneness experiences, the boundaries of perception bend and dissolve. We can physically feel what we normally think. We can see what we normally hear. Things that are solid become permeable.

I first experienced this kind of fluidity at age seventeen, returning from a weekend retreat. The retreat had been difficult and, I thought, ineffective. By Sunday evening, I felt grumpy and miserable as I climbed into the bus to Dublin. I found an empty window seat and plonked my bag on the seat next to me, a warning to anyone foolish enough to think about getting friendly and spoiling my misery.

While waiting for the driver to start the engine, I was overcome by a sense of peace so strong I could touch it. This peace was physical, like the air had become solid in my hands yet was still air at the same time. I breathed peace, touched it, submerged myself in it. I needed nothing more than to simply be where I was right then. For the first time, I understood what the Bible calls a "peace that passes understanding," that a reality existed beyond what I knew, a universe beyond my normal perception.

Sometimes oneness experiences feel like falling into a void. I lived in New Mexico for a year. Many times, while driving across the Rio Grande River, I had the sensation of falling through the bridge. It wasn't a psychotic losing-touch-with-reality feeling, but more that I was inhabiting two realities at the same time. I wasn't afraid because

I thought I was falling into the river; I was afraid because I *was* falling into an inner void.

Greek philosopher Plato's famous analogy of a cave is probably the best way to describe this kind of oneness state. The people in Plato's cave saw shadows on one of the cave walls and thought what they saw was reality. St. Paul of the Damascus Road conversion called this "looking through a glass darkly." When crossing the Rio Grande, I sometimes felt as if I had passed through that dark glass into reality, only my reality was emptiness, a void. A void is not pleasant to most people, so it can be accompanied by fear, anxiety, or an intense feeling of aloneness. Because of this, we can easily label these events as bad experiences to be avoided and, if they're persistent, to be medicated away. However, if we don't panic and we hold off on the medication, that void can become full to overflowing with objectless, sourceless love, a very comfortable place to rest.

Here's a description of the awakening of what in the Hindu tradition is called "kundalini energy." Kundalini life energy is usually depicted as a dormant serpent coiled at the base of the spine. When the serpent awakens, it soars upward, blasting open all the energy centers in the body, also known as chakras.

This is how Hannah, another client, described her experience with kundalini: "I was traveling by myself in the United States. I went to visit someone I had worked for years earlier when I was a student. He was talking to me, making jokes. It was nice, like the years since we'd last met had just fallen away. Then I felt this heat in my lower back. I didn't pay much attention until it started creeping up my spine. It freaked me out. I kept telling myself to stay calm, nobody could see it, it would pass. But it didn't. It just got stronger and stronger until it came right up my spine. It felt like it was gushing out of the top of my head. Then it was amazing. Every cell in my body felt so alive, like they were reaching out for sensation. My lips, the backs of my hands, my arms, everything tingled with aliveness. Even my vision was clearer. I was merged with, I don't know, life itself. I *was* life, and nothing was impossible. I could do anything. I could move mountains if I wanted to, but all I wanted was to sit there and enjoy it." Hannah's kundalini experience lasted six weeks.

At the time of this experience, Hannah was less than a year out of a twenty-year relationship. Her partner had initiated the breakup and insisted that the split was final, with no hope of reconciliation. Hannah couldn't accept that. She couldn't let go, couldn't move on. She described this as a prison from which she saw no escape. Her kundalini experience shattered that prison. In that one evening, she let go of her relationship, her partner, her terror of a future without him. Five years on from it, she still insists it was one of the major turning points in her life.

Oneness is a deeply personal, internal experience. Its manifestations vary with each individual. In the case of Angela, it appeared as the dissolving of physical forms—she could grasp the sky. For Hannah, her intense physical energy blasted her into union with life itself. Lisa experienced a love that drove out the fear separating her from her classmates, while I experienced peace as the air I breathed. But these are just fingers pointing to the moon. The core mystical experience, oneness, goes beyond words and images, shapes and forms. Oneness is pure, vital, vibrant existence. And it has a long history.

ONENESS THROUGH THE AGES AND ACROSS CULTURES

Abraham Maslow's term "peak state" refers to an expansion of awareness. The phenomenon of expanded awareness has a history that spans several millennia and almost all cultures and traditions. It has many other names, my favorite being the more poetic "mystical experience," or mysticism. When we describe these experiences as peak states, it can give the impression that they are isolated events that can be induced by certain practices or by drugs. When we describe them as mystical, we set them into a much broader, life-encompassing tradition of spirituality. Mystical experience is intrinsic to human existence, and the tradition of mysticism stretches back through time and transcends cultures and civilizations.

Indigenous native cultures are often called pagan. But pagan native cultures lived close to nature and developed a rich, lived spirituality. Most indigenous societies had shamans, also known as healers, medicine men/women, or witch doctors. The source of a shaman's powers as a healer lay in his or her encounter with the mystical, with the world beyond the shapes and forms of everyday reality. In the early stages of a shaman's development, encounters with the mystical could be troubled and difficult, often resembling what modern psychiatrists would call severe depression or even psychosis.

During his journey into states of expanded awareness, the shaman often suffered attacks by devils, evil spirits, monsters, or animals. The shamanic journey into other realities has parallels in all the major religions. Jesus went into the desert alone to be goaded and tempted by the devil. Mohammed was left deeply troubled by his vision of the angel Gabriel, the event that marked the beginning of his life as the great prophet and founder of Islam. Buddha had to contend with the mythical Mara, who showered him with swords and arrows. We can take these fearsome devils and monsters literally, or we can see them as the mythical, culturally shaped personifications of aspects of the human psyche. It matters little, because the important part of the story is that out of this encounter with other realities come transformation and awakening to new life.

The value of this journey beyond the ordinary has been recognized in most societies and religions, so much so that the experience has been induced through various forms of ritual and endurance. Indigenous societies used ritual dancing, chanting, and drumming to induce nonordinary levels of awareness. Native American and Aboriginal cultures used the vision quest and the walkabout, where, like Jesus, young people go into the wilderness alone for extended periods of time. In Greco-Roman civilization, groups and practices like the Temple of Isis, the Bacchanalian Rites of Dionysus, or the Orphic cult were devoted to pushing people beyond ordinary consciousness. Some of the initiations involved the use of drugs such as ayahuasca or alcohol as well as practices modern society would find repulsive, but they were, at least at the start, intended to break through the world of forms and shapes into a greater reality.

Mystical groups can also be found within the major organized religions. Within Islam, the Sufis use the spinning of the dervishes as the experiential route into union with Allah. The various schools of yoga and tantra within Hinduism offer direct experience of transcendence through postures, breathing, and awareness. Buddhism has its own tantric and Zen strains, and Judaism has the Kabbalah. Christianity has the "desert fathers and mothers" of the third century, mystics who chose to live in the deserts of Egypt and North Africa. Christianity also has a lineage of mystic saints, such as St. Teresa of Avila, St. John of the Cross, and Julian of Norwich. And then came the Enlightenment.

The intellectual movement known as the Enlightenment spread across Europe and the American colonies in the late seventeenth century. It was a movement of liberation: liberation from kings, from superstition, from what Enlightenment philosophers saw as antiquated thinking. Many of the political and economic freedoms we enjoy today have their roots in Enlightenment philosophy. But the movement was a two-edged sword.

The catchphrase of the Enlightenment, *Cogito ergo sum* ("I think, therefore I am"), heralded the Age of Reason. From the Enlightenment on, the rational, reasoning mind became our guide to truth. Reliance on objective, scientific inquiry as the touchstone of reality took root in society, and as a result, whatever we couldn't test, measure, and quantify became suspect. That included mysticism.

The Enlightenment brought a much-needed break from superstition, but it would take nearly 150 years for mystical experience to regain its credibility in the West. That recovery took off in the period after World War II. In 1954, renowned writer Aldous Huxley published his book *The Doors of Perception*, about his experiences with the drug mescaline. Ten years later, respected psychologist Abraham Maslow published *Religions, Values and Peak-Experiences*. In that book, Maslow used the term "peak experience" to describe the kind of extraordinary spiritual experiences Huxley, among others, had written about. Around this time, too, LSD became a popular drug both inside and outside of psychiatric institutions. Through Huxley, Timothy Leary, Richard Alpert (Ram Dass), the beatnik poets, and the LSD phenomenon, the counterculture movement was born. At the same time, Christian mystics Anthony de Mello and Thomas Merton published books on spirituality that still sell well today. During this period, the West also discovered yoga, meditation, and New Age spirituality. Once again, people began to explore mystical experiences.

So far, scientific investigation into the phenomenon of mystical experience has been limited. We do know that mystical states are associated with changes in brain wave frequency—moving from the beta wave pattern of normal waking state consciousness to theta and delta waves associated with deep meditation, trance states, and access to the unconscious mind. Mystical states are also associated with a reduction in activity in the outer part of the brain (the cortex) and an increase in activity in the older, inner regions of the brain.

The outer layers of the brain are used for reasoning, language, and conceptualization. The older, inner regions are associated with emotionality and sensory and nonverbal experience. Increased activity here, combined with a reduction of activity in the cognitive centers, could account for some of the features of the mystical state— the melting away of boundaries and forms and the raw, immediate engagement with life unmediated by words and thoughts.[5,6]

But more research is needed. The difficulty with scientific investigation lies in the fact that a mystical experience is completely subjective and defies description, thus creating a problem with objective verification. Why then should we look to spiritual experience for guidance in the real and tangible task of navigating daily life?

Ken Wilber, in his book *A Brief History of Everything,* offers an answer to this question. Wilber writes: "Spirit transcends all, so it includes all. It is utterly beyond this world, but utterly embraces every single holon in this world ... It's the highest rung in the ladder, but it's also the wood out of which the entire ladder is made."[7] In other words, we cannot avoid the spiritual; we can only remain unaware of it. It is who we are, and it is the matrix in which we move and live. Two thousand or so years ago, the Bible put it more poetically: spirit is the "ground in which we live and move and have our being" (Acts 17:28). Spirit is the nature of our universe, the essence of who we are. And, as we shall see, when it comes to living our lives to the fullest, mystical experiences are among our greatest teachers.

EXERCISE 1: RECOGNIZING MYSTICAL EXPERIENCES

Review your own life. Check the box if you have experienced any of the following without the aid of drugs:

- ❑ Feeling in the flow, absorbed in a task
- ❑ Feeling vibrantly alive, tingling with aliveness
- ❑ Feeling fully, totally present in any situation
- ❑ Feeling merged with your partner during sex
- ❑ Feeling merged with nature or marveling at the wonder of nature
- ❑ Feeling all-consuming joy
- ❑ Seeing shapes and colors more vividly than usual
- ❑ Feeling unconditional love, acceptance, trust

❑ Feeling totally free

❑ Knowing intuitively what is the right thing to do, the right path to take

If you said yes to any of these, you may have experienced a state of expanded awareness. You may even have experienced the merging-with-life feeling that is called oneness. The state may have occurred spontaneously. In the chapters and exercises that follow, we will look at ways you can open yourself to having more and more of these life-enhancing mystical experiences.

2

THE FIVE PRACTICES

Pulling out the chair
Beneath your mind
And watching you fall upon God—
~HAFIZ

"Now grab the other sleeve with your left hand and pull it over your shoulder," Maureen ordered.

Andrew stood at the front of the room, his right arm stuck fully into the sleeve of his jacket. The other sleeve hung behind his shoulder, dangling almost to his knees. He smiled for his audience, reached for the limp sleeve with his left hand, and pulled it over his right shoulder.

"No! No!" Maureen snapped. "Pull it behind your neck to your other shoulder."

"Well, why didn't you say that the first time?"

Five minutes earlier, the exercise had seemed so simple, and Maureen and Andrew had jumped at the chance to take part. The group of ten community organizers had come to my class to learn about basic communication skills. After Andrew finally managed to get into his own jacket, we analyzed the experience.

Maureen's job was to tell Andrew how to put on the jacket. Andrew's job was to follow exactly what Maureen said, nothing more and nothing less. The key to success in this exercise is for both people to empty their minds of everything they already know about putting on a coat.

Andrew, by my estimation, had about forty years' experience donning various coats and jackets. After the first few years of practice, the mechanics of dressing ourselves become automatic—something we know so completely, we don't even think about it. Maureen's jacketing experience spanned approximately twenty-five years, which was not quite as much as Andrew, but more than enough for her to "know" how to do it unconsciously.

For Maureen to instruct effectively, she had to see the task with a "beginner's mind." If she couldn't do this, she wouldn't be able to break down her instructions into the tiny, precise steps necessary to communicate with Andrew. To follow her instructions accurately, Andrew, too, had to empty his mind of decades of experience and "knowing." He had to listen to what was being said rather than fill in the gaps with his own store of knowledge.

The analysis that day focused on communications: how everything is filtered through our minds and often altered substantially in the process; how we assume people know what we're saying, so we leave out essential details. But the exercise struck me as an equally good illustration of the biggest obstacle we face on our path to oneness: our own minds.

It's an Experience

Spirituality is an experience of connection with the essence of life. Some people call this essence "God." Others refer to it as the divine, or spirit, or the cosmos, or a host of other names. However we characterize it, spirituality transcends who we are as individuals and unites us with something greater than ourselves.

Mysticism is a branch of spirituality. Mystics use states of expanded consciousness to become aware of realities beyond the visible material world of our daily lives. A mystical state is an experience—a deep, profound, all-encompassing experience of the realities that lie beyond the grasp of ordinary awareness.

The core of a mystical state is the experience of union, or oneness. Because of the way we shape our universe, when we use the terms "union" and "oneness," it's natural to ask, union with what? Oneness with what? The answer people usually give is oneness with mystery, with self, with nature, with a deity, or beyond deity, with emptiness itself. The experience of oneness is also described as going into the light, enlightenment, or transcendence. But in this experience, there is no "with." Oneness is a state of being, not an action, and definitions fall so far short of the real experience that many of the best-known mystics—Rumi, Hafiz, John of the Cross—found mere prose a woefully inadequate tool to describe the reality of oneness. They did, instead, use poetry, often beautiful poetry replete with sexual imagery and metaphor, the poetry of the Song of Solomon in the Bible, for example.

This makes states of oneness difficult to comprehend with the normal processes of the mind. When we encounter something new, we naturally compare it to what we already know. We analyze and assess it within the limits of our existing store of knowledge, which is usually a useful way to go about learning and adapting to new things. However, mystical experiences go so far beyond what we already "know" that, as with Maureen and Andrew, and Damian from the introduction, eventually our store of trusted knowledge about the world can become more of a hindrance than a help. As Buddhist writer Pema Chödrön says, "Letting there be room for not knowing is the most important thing of all."[8]

This field demands a healthy scepticism. It also demands an openness to wonder and a willingness to jump into the unknown and uncharted. Sooner or later we have to let go of what we know with our intellect. We have to pull the chair from under our own mind. This is a prerequisite to discovering the all-encompassing, multi-dimensional reality that lies beyond mere "knowing."

EXERCISE 2: SUSPENDING MIND MEDITATION

Read these instructions before beginning.

Find yourself a comfortable place where you can be alone and uninterrupted for at least ten minutes. Then find an object to look at. A piece of furniture such as a chair or table would be a good choice. Sit within touching distance of your chosen object. Let's say it's a chair.

- Place one hand on your belly and take ten slow breaths that fill your belly and expand your chest. While you're doing this, focus your attention on the sensation of air going in and out of your lungs, on the movement of your chest and belly.

- Take ten more slow breaths, but this time focus your attention on the chair before you, letting go of all distractions.

- Scan the chair slowly with your eyes. Follow the shape of its legs without making any judgments about those legs—no inner comment about curves and angles, no judgments about whether you like their shape or not, whether they are in good condition or not. No commentary whatsoever. Just observe the legs of the chair.

- Move your eyes upward. Take in the seat, the back, the arms, if there are any. Linger on each curve, each angle. Linger on the texture of the material from which the chair is made, the texture and pattern of the upholstery fabric, if there is any. But again, no inner comment, no likes and dislikes. Just look. Receive the image of the chair as it is, without judgment.

- Move on to touching the chair. Feel the textures, the angles, the sweep of curves, the softness or hardness of cushions. Just feel. Let the textures come to you through your fingers. Let them fill your awareness.

- When you have completed your scan of the object, sit back, relax, and think about how your experience of the object differs from the way you normally "see." What did it feel like to observe something, to receive it into your awareness, without judgment or comment? Did you see anything about the object that you had not noticed before? Did you experience any changes in your perception— perhaps more vivid colors or deeper textures?

If you feel ready, you can extend this exercise into more challenging areas. However, the objects suggested here are likely to provoke some emotional responses. Before proceeding, you need to feel ready to experience these emotional responses and be skilled at handling them.

One of the most challenging objects for this exercise is your own face in a mirror, or your own body. You can also perform the exercise with photos of friends or loved ones, or you can work directly with a friend or loved one and scan each other's faces. However, if you are not comfortable doing this kind of intimate, personal work with a friend, you are likely to end up laughing and joking. This in itself is not a bad thing, but it's not the exercise.

So What?

With the exception of St. Paul's conversion, all the oneness experiences described in chapter 1 come from the lives of ordinary people. As we've seen, oneness experiences are common, and not just among people who meditate regularly or engage in other spiritual techniques. They are usually moving and pleasant events, but they can pass. And no matter how profound and beautiful the experience is, you still have to get up in the morning, brush your teeth, feed the kids, pay the mortgage, etc. Life goes on, and spiritual experiences don't alter that fact. What they do alter is us, and the nature of how we engage with life.

Mystical experiences teach us how to show up for life in a way that makes our living gritty, substantial, and satisfying. This is not the same as living pain-free, although it can greatly reduce our suffering. Nor is it the same as experiencing material success, although it can include that kind of success. It does mean that whatever we do, we do it 100 percent, totally honest, fully committed, heart and soul. No hedging bets, no pulling punches.

For many people, full engagement living is synonymous with a jam-packed, hectic lifestyle. That's true for some, but we can also be fully engaged with life when we're alone, doing nothing at all, or carrying out the most mundane of daily tasks. Either way, full engagement with life can be a scary prospect because it involves stepping out into the unknown. Because being fully present means that we give up our mental chatter, even sitting alone in an empty room can be difficult. Mental chatter can be comforting, like a heavy blanket wrapped around us that we have gotten so used to, we barely know it's there. Without that blanket of noise, we must face what may lie beneath it, what we don't know. Whether our lifestyle is hectic or sedate, or anything in between, we can be fully engaged with life only if we feel safe enough to do so. And we feel safe if we know we are alchemists who have a foolproof system of turning anything life puts in our way into spiritual gold. Mystical experience offers just such a system.

Another word for meditation is "contemplation," and spiritual writers often talk about the "contemplative mind." The **contemplative mind** is the approach to life that we develop as our spiritual awareness grows. The contemplative mind sees life as a rich harvest of experience, and every experience, whether pleasant or painful, is fuel for spiritual growth. When we engage with life from the perspective of the contemplative mind, everything we encounter in life becomes the means through which we grow, through which we open ourselves to infinite love.

The contemplative mind's way of engaging with life can be broken down into five approaches, or practices. In real time, these practices function together as one, but we will look at them under five headings.

Practice 1: Radical Awareness

Practice 2: Living in the Present

Practice 3: Trust and Openness

Practice 4: Growing from Adversity

Practice 5: Oneness (also known as Nondualism)

These practices are not just ways of thinking, they are ways of living every day and every moment. They can transform the way we think and act and feel, and they can liberate us from the mental and emotional conditioning that sets the perimeter of our lives.

A New Testament parable tells the story of a farmer scattering seed onto various kinds of soil. Seed that falls on stony soil doesn't grow well. All of us can enter mystical states, but for the experience to take root and grow, most of us need to do some soil tilling. Soil tilling, in this instance, is the inner work of clearing out emotional baggage, of opening our minds and reclaiming lost parts of ourselves, and it usually falls under the label "psychology." There is no artificial separation of the spiritual from the psychological, and psychological work is part of our spiritual journey. The wisdom of oneness experiences, distilled into the five practices, is our companion and our guide to psychological as well as spiritual growth.

In the chapters that follow, we are going to examine the five practices in detail, using exercises to help us gain proficiency in each practice. Then, in part 2, we are going to apply these practices to some of the greatest internal obstacles we face when we set ourselves on the path to full engagement living.

3

THE FIRST PRACTICE:
Radical Awareness

*But tragically, most people never get to see
that all is well because they are asleep.*
~ANTHONY DE MELLO

I once paid a client a compliment. I told him the jacket he wore to a therapy session was lovely. I expected maybe a thank you or perhaps a grunt. Instead, his whole body stiffened, and he glared at me with fire in his eyes. When I finally got him to talk, I discovered anger was a mild word for the rage he felt toward me in that moment. This tall, handsome man's self-esteem was so low, he went through life believing he was defective in every way—physically, intellectually, and emotionally. When I complimented him, he believed I was lying, with the intention of making a fool of him.

This was the muddy filter through which he saw the world, and it shaped the quality of his life on every level. He fully expected people to reject him. Focused on insult, he couldn't recognize a compliment, and when someone sincerely reached out to him, he reacted with rage. Not surprisingly, he didn't have a lot of friends.

THE SMALL SELF

When we are very young, life speaks to us all the time through the people around us. In the eyes of others, we learn how loved or unloved we are, what is good and not so good about us, how attractive or unattractive we are. We often interpret things people say and do as comments on ourselves, then we bend and shape ourselves accordingly. We find out what works, and we adapt. The "lessons" we learn about how to survive in life become the patterns by which we interact with the world. This process is called conditioning.

Conditioning shapes what spiritual writers sometimes refer to as our "Small Self." British psychologist Donald Winnicott described the development of our Small Self, which he called a "false self," throughout infancy and childhood. Our Small Self is our personality, our likes and dislikes, our self-image, and our patterns of relating to life and each other. Our Small Self interacts with the world. It filters our awareness and colors everything we see. When someone asks us to describe ourselves, what we describe is our Small Self.

In forensic psychology, it's generally accepted that eyewitness testimony is notoriously unreliable because witnesses, like all of us, see through the filter of patterns they already know. If what we're looking at doesn't match what we expect to find, we fill in the gaps. In other words, how we see determines what we see.[9] We all do this. We all look at the world through the lens of our Small Self. That lens can be murky indeed. Spiritual growth demands a much clearer vision.

THE BIG SELF

This clear vision, vision free from Small Self conditioning, is called awareness. Awareness is spiritual literacy, the fundamental skill of the contemplative mind, and it's a function of the Big Self (also called the True Self, Essential Self, Divine Self). The Big and Small Selves are not "things" in themselves, but levels of awareness. Big Self awareness is greater than, but includes, the level of awareness we call the Small Self.

We operate out of our Big Self when we are directly, nakedly experiencing, when we are too busy *being* to engage in analyzing who we are. Our Big Self is truly, unselfconsciously present to what is happening right now. There is no place here for the defensiveness or the filters of the Small Self. We step into this Big Self during mystical experiences.

The limitations of our conditioning and personal history fall away when we enter a oneness state. During a oneness experience, we can feel as if we've been sprung from a box that has been part of our life for so long, we didn't even know it was there. When we see without filters, the view is astonishing. On a physical level, visual perception changes. I often slipped into expanded awareness when facilitating breathwork sessions. While I watched clients breathe, their faces seemed to change before my eyes. The creases and tensions etched into their features melted away. But more than that, their personality, the shape into which life had sculpted them, seemed to dissolve, and the essence of who they were emerged into the room. When we see this clearly, a new reality emerges. As British poet William Blake put it, "If the doors of perception were cleansed, everything would appear to man as it is, infinite."

On an emotional level, oneness experiences are states of great compassion, joy, and peace. Hurt, anger, and resentment all pale in significance next to the shimmering beauty at the heart of everything. Our battles with others, our concerns with being right or wrong, our image or any of the other issues we get caught up in day to day, melt into the deep assurance that "all shall be well, and all shall be well." [10] This is Big Self awareness, radical awareness.

That same deep compassion prevails when we turn the light of awareness on ourselves on a daily basis. Which is a good thing, because this "waking up" to reality [11] demands honest self-reflection. Awareness brings us face to face with aspects of ourselves that can be embarrassing or shameful. The only way to manage this is to accept ourselves without judgment and without our Small Self defenses. If we are to transcend the obstacles that keep us from embracing our lives fully, we must embrace the state and skill of Big Self awareness.

Developing Awareness

Let's begin with something that operates during most people's every waking moment: visual perception. Stare at the picture in the following figure for a few minutes. What do you see? Sprays of white radiating forward over a black spiral? Or a central white spiral surrounded by sprays of white? If the picture doesn't change from a black spiral to white, keep staring at it. Notice what happens in your mind just as you switch from one perspective to another. Keep staring through several changes of perspective until you've pinned down what's going on in your mind. Then read on.

The harder you try to find a shape in the picture, the less likely you are to find one. Once we begin to impose patterns or search for interpretations, awareness is lost. The key is to stop trying and just let your eyes rest on what's before you. Then a new perspective emerges. This is a simple exercise in non-judgmental awareness, an exercise in suspending our thinking and allowing what is before us to emerge.

To get to the level of Big Self awareness, one part of us must stand back and observe the rest of us. This part that can stand back, that can observe our inner and outer workings, is called our "Inner Witness." Initially, this Inner Witness is an observer of our day-to-day experience in retrospect. We can practice retrospective awareness by looking back on something that occurred recently. A good example comes from a former client, Paula.

PAULA AND HER INNER WITNESS

Paula worked in a busy office and sometimes felt overwhelmed by the volume of work. She prided herself on being good at her job, but as we talked, it became obvious that time management was not her strong point. She arrived for her fourth session angry and distressed.

The previous day, she had forgotten to process an important order for a customer. The customer lost money, and Paula's supervisor had to do a lot of groveling to retain the account. Paula was called into the supervisor's office and told exactly what her mistake had cost the company. She listened in silence, then wasted the rest of the day replaying events over and over in her mind. By five o'clock she had convinced herself that she was overworked, undersupported, and not appreciated, and the mistake was no big deal anyway. That evening she included friends and family in her little scenario. She carefully crafted the story in such a way that they took her side and told her what a terrible person her supervisor was and how she shouldn't put up with such bad treatment. By bedtime she'd concluded that her supervisor was jealous of her.

Paula's Inner Witness hadn't been seen in a long time, but the detached Inner Witness perspective was just what she needed to get beyond the anger she'd been nurturing for the previous two days. A good starting point in an emotionally charged situation is the emotion itself. We used slow, deep breathing to help Paula focus her awareness on the anger she felt in her body. She was about to resurrect her Inner Witness.

The Inner Witness moves through ever deepening layers of awareness by simply observing—nothing else, just observing. It doesn't judge. Right and wrong don't enter into things. In fact, right and wrong only cloud awareness. The Inner Witness doesn't interpret either. It's tempting to psychoanalyze others, to work out why they do what they do. But this is a ruse, an escape route for ourselves so we can deflect our attention from our own motivations and behavior. The Inner Witness never feeds the emotion with action replays of what happened, and it doesn't fast-forward into what might happen in the future.

It took only a few minutes for Paula to discover a fundamental truth: awareness changes everything. Once she became fully aware of her anger, it lost its potency. Awareness does this; it takes the sting out of our feelings. When her anger dissolved, another, far more difficult emotion emerged: shame.

Shame had rooted itself a lot more deeply in Paula's body, but the role of the Inner Witness is the same at all levels of awareness: to simply observe without judgment in present time. Through tears and a lot of deep breathing (more about breathwork in chapter 6), Paula broke through the screen of her emotions to find the source of her shame: a core belief that she was deeply flawed. Anger and blame were her default defenses against the shame of being wrong, imperfect. Paula continued deep breathing until she touched the point where anger and shame, right and wrong, all dissolve into a single point of complete stillness.

On a practical level, awareness liberated Paula from hours of emotional suffering, hours of time wasted justifying her behavior to herself and to anyone else who would listen. It broke her old cycle of anger and blame. From that point on, Paula had options: She could do something about her workload and her nonexistent time-management skills. She could become more effective at her job.

Small Self thinking can be categorized in several ways. The following table shows Paula's Small Self thinking broken down into categories, her thoughts, and the influence her thinking exercised over her emotions and behavior.

PAULA'S SMALL SELF THINKING		
CATEGORY	THOUGHTS	EFFECTS
Core Beliefs Deep-seated beliefs we hold about ourselves and life.	I'm wrong. I should be perfect.	Shame so intense it has to be avoided through blame and anger. Blame and anger prevent her from looking at her situation realistically and doing something about it.

PAULA'S SMALL SELF THINKING (CONT.)		
CATEGORY	THOUGHTS	EFFECTS
Image Identifying with a characteristic you display to the world.	I'm very good at my job. It's important to be good at a job. It's who I am, and people respect me for it.	Paula equates what she does with who she is. She's so tied up with preserving her image as an exemplary employee that she's blind to her own shortcomings and therefore blocked from finding a solution to the problem.
Mask Closely aligned with image, this is a characteristic or role that we hide behind.	I'm a nice person. I'm responsible and work hard.	Prevented her from speaking up about her workload. Allowed her to blame others and therefore not see or take responsibility for her own role in the problem and its solution.
Blame To throw responsibility for something onto others.	The customer should have gotten his act together. He left it too late to place his order. My supervisor should be able to see how overworked I am.	Paula is completely focused outside herself for both the cause and the solution. She is disempowering herself through blaming others. The customer and supervisor may have played a part in caus-ing the problem, but focusing on them exclusively means Paula is powerless to change anything. Responsibility creates personal power. Blame creates helplessness.

PAULA'S SMALL SELF THINKING		
CATEGORY	THOUGHTS	EFFECTS
Victim Mentality Seeing yourself as a victim of circumstances or of the behavior of others ("them").	I'm taking the blame for their incompetence. The customer can do whatever he likes—"they" never say anything to him.	Paula is now completely powerless to do anything because there's no point. No matter what she does, "they" will never change and they have all the power.
Projection Seeing in others what is really in ourselves.	The customer can't get anything done on time. He's useless, and then he blames me.	Avoids facing being wrong herself, both in the present situation and as a core belief about herself as a human being. Avoids having to face her own shortcomings in terms of time management. If she doesn't face these issues in herself, she will never be able to do anything about them.
Psychologizing Analyzing the motivations of others. Particularly strong in people who know some psychology or have amassed a lot of spiritual knowledge.	My supervisor is jealous of me.	Justifies her behavior and her anger. Allows her to focus on other people instead of herself and her own empowerment through taking responsibility for her own actions.

Paula's deepest feelings and beliefs lay buried beneath multiple layers of defenses. Awareness is not about using our intellect to chart and analyze these defenses. Awareness is the act of being present, not doing; it is being, without doing anything. Insight comes when we let what is before us emerge. This happens only when we are fully present without judgment or expectation.

When Paula's Inner Witness brought shame to the surface, Paula could approach her job differently, through her Big Self awareness. Here is a summary of how Paula's Big Self saw her work situation, as well as the effect that change of perspective had on Paula.

PAULA'S BIG SELF THINKING	
THOUGHTS	EFFECTS
I made a mistake and that's normal. Nothing in this situation is shameful to me or anyone else.	Relief eliminates blame and criticism of herself and anyone else. She no longer has to justify to herself what she did by making other people wrong. It is much easier now to see how to handle the situation constructively.
The mistake happened because I am not managing my work efficiently, and I sometimes have too much work.	Can now see that she needs skills training to help her manage her time efficiently. She can also recognize the need to speak up when work gets overwhelming.
I freely choose to do this job. I am responsible for doing it to the best of my ability.	Gives her the responsibility and therefore the power to change the way she does the job through assertiveness and time-management skills.
I have the power to make changes that would ease my burdens.	Gives her the option to take action instead of being a victim at the mercy of "them."

EXERCISE 3: MY SMALL SELF THINKING/
MY BIG SELF THINKING

Choose a situation in your life that you'd like to improve. For now, pick something that's not too emotionally charged. Find a place to be alone and bring along a pen and paper. Put the heading "My Small Self Thinking" at the top of the first page, and divide the page into two columns. Label the left-hand column "Thoughts" and the right-hand column "Effects." Put the heading "My Big Self Thinking" at the top of the second page, and divide that page into two columns with the same labels as the first page.

Get comfortable and breathe slowly and deeply. Follow your breath with your mind. Focus on the inhale as cool air enters your body and on the exhale as warm air exits. Feel the physical pleasure of breathing. Then let the situation that's troubling you enter your awareness. Stare at it the way you stared at the spirals and sprays in the figure earlier in this chapter. Hold the situation in your awareness without thinking about it. Just hold it in your awareness and see what your Inner Witness brings forth.

Using Paula's Small Self template from this chapter as a guide, write down your own Small Self beliefs about the situation you've chosen to examine in the first column. Don't worry about categorizing them. You can do that later, if you want. When you've finished writing, review your list. Then take the time to honestly work out how those Small Self beliefs influence your actions and reactions. Write your ideas in the second column.

Turn to your second page. Follow the breathing instructions again until you feel calm and anchored in yourself. Invite your Inner Witness to guide you to Big Self thinking. Review your situation from the detached Big Self perspective, the perspective of your Inner Witness. Then write down your Big Self thoughts in the first column. When you have completed your list, ask yourself, "If I were to operate out of my Big Self in this situation, what would change?" Write your answers in the second column. Use Paula's Big Self thinking template as a guide. Could you implement any of those Big Self approaches in your life?

AWARENESS IN REAL TIME

As we become more skilled at self-observation, the Inner Witness begins to operate in real time rather than after the fact. We spot ourselves getting caught up in our old ways *while* we are getting caught up in them. This is an important development because it means we can recognize and change our behavior in the moment. We can calm anger, say "yes" instead of "no" or vice versa. We can decline to engage in the same old arguments that end up the same old way. This is a nice change from analyzing what we should have done and should have said after the opportunity to do or say anything has passed. The Inner Witness, operating in present time, is what gives us the space to see and transcend our conditioning.

Spiritual techniques such as breathwork or meditation bring our Inner Witness to life. They teach us to observe the contents of our mind. We watch thoughts come and go without following them with our attention, without interpreting or analyzing them, without acting on them. The more we practice awareness, the more we wake up to the reality of ourselves and others without the filter of our own fears, masks, patterns, or beliefs. Awareness without filters is radical awareness. Radical awareness changes the way we see the world. It teaches us to engage with life as it is rather than how we think it is or want it to be. And then radical awareness takes us further.

The ancient Celts celebrated what they called Samhain. Christians called it All Hallows' Eve. We call it Halloween. (Modern Pagans still celebrate Samhain.) According to Celtic tradition, at Samhain, the veil between our world of concrete forms and shapes grows thin and we can pass through it into the wider spiritual world beyond ordinary consciousness, the world of oneness. But we don't have to wait until Samhain to experience oneness with life. Radical awareness takes us through that veil into the heart of our spiritual nature.

To be aware, we need our Inner Witness. But if we try to describe this Inner Witness, we realize it has no attributes—no gender, no character or personality, no likes or dislikes, no history. The Inner Witness is our Big, True, Divine Self. Our Big Self opens up a reality that is far more liberating and fulfilling than anything sleep can bring.

4

THE SECOND AND THIRD PRACTICES:
Living in the Present with Trust and Openness

Yesterday is gone.
Tomorrow has not yet come.
We have only today.
Let us begin.
~MOTHER TERESA

I am a future thinker. Over the years, I've spent large chunks of time thinking about what will happen a few hours, a week, a year, ten years from now. This valuable trait means I can see ahead. I can plan and organize, and in my work, I've often been able to spot trends coming when others could not. This skill has served me well, most of the time. But during some periods in my life—all of my teens and twenties, in fact—living in the future robbed me of decades of real time. I have a good friend who has spent most of his life looking backward, ruminating and obsessing over all the little things he said, didn't say, should have said. He has a finely tuned ability to review his past. The skill has brought him some insight and wisdom, but for him, as for me, too much time spent outside the present constitutes a waste of precious days.

Lots of us are either future or past thinkers. We spend varying amounts of time living somewhere other than where we are now. Whatever advantages there are to being able to remember the past or project into the future, neither will bring us anywhere near the exquisite richness of the present moment—where life is located. Being in the present, the *now*, not a second in the past or a second in the future, is a feature of all meditation. A common denominator of oneness experiences, both mine and those of my clients, was that they all took place in the now. We entered the present moment deliberately through breathwork or various other forms of meditation, or it happened spontaneously. Either way, the now it was.

In a state of oneness, the present is eternal. There is only now, and now teems with life. The now is an invaluable resource for helping us deal effectively with whatever life brings. But one of the biggest walls between us and the now is the constant stream of chatter going on in our own minds.

THE WALL OF SOUND

I once shared a hotel room with a woman who gave voice to every thought that passed through her head. We had both signed on for a three-week tour of Australia and ended up sharing accommodations.

"I'm falling asleep," my roommate announced every night as she lay in bed. "No … my ankle is itchy. Oooo, that's a lovely scratch. Nothing like a good scratch. What makes things itchy? Maybe the cloth …"

Some people talk to themselves out loud. It's their way of working through tasks and problems. Most of us talk to ourselves silently in the form of an endless stream of thoughts. According to the Laboratory of Neuro Imaging at the University of Southern California, the average person has around 70,000 thoughts per day.[12] My roommate gave voice to every single one of her 70,000. But the same stream of thought, silent and invisible, goes on inside our own heads every waking moment. Because my roommate thought out loud, for the first time I could actually see the effect a person's inner dialogue could have on their experience of life.

For the most part, the content of her monologue was benign. Not so her process of thinking. The stream of chatter acted as a barrier between her and direct, unmediated contact with the world, like tourists who are so focused on taking photographs that they experience life through a camera instead of firsthand.

Mind chatter is not always as innocent as my roommate's running commentary on her itchy ankles. It's often about things that have already happened or that may happen in the future. Not only does this take us away from what's happening right now, but many of us compound the problem by catastrophizing. We anticipate the worst possible outcomes. We paint word pictures in our mind that are so convincing, we work ourselves up to believing the worst has already happened. Catastrophizing mind chatter feeds anxiety and an underlying tendency to worry.

Another equally destructive form of mind chatter is analysis. Those of us who are prone to analysis dissect situations and relationships. We pick apart what we think are the underlying motivations and feelings in an interaction and analyze what the other person "really" meant. Again, the chatter becomes so convincing that we believe our own analysis. Mind chatter creates a world within our minds that we take to be reality.

In the '60s, music producer Phil Spector developed something he called the "wall of sound." In some of the best songs of the era, the wall of sound rose up gradually until it enveloped the listener, completely surrounding them with music. Mind chatter builds a wall of words that's just as enveloping as Spector's wall of sound. This wall of words can insulate us from reality and, at the same time, convince us that what we have conjured up in our minds is reality.

Silencing the Chatter: An Experiment in Being Present

Meditation techniques are designed to help silence the inner chatter, or at least to offer reprieve from it. Meditation falls into two broad categories: techniques designed to empty the mind of all thought, and techniques that allow the flow of thoughts to continue, but instead of getting caught up in them, we watch them float by. When meditating for the first time, it's common to expect immediate inner silence, so anything less can seem like failure. That's not the way meditation works. It goes more like this:

Right now, writing this chapter, I'm sitting in a pink room. I love the room. I love the intense color of the walls. I take a deep, slow breath, then another, focusing on the sensation of breathing. Silence ensues, perhaps a whole second of it before my mind resumes its buzz. My mind is full of ideas. I silence the thinking again and stare at the wall. "I'm silent now," I tell myself. That, of course, is chatter. Silence prevails again, maybe two seconds this time. I begin to notice textures in the wall surface and promptly tell myself I'm noticing textures—more chatter. This goes on for a bit until I engage more fully with my breathing. Finally, for moments at a time, I come fully into the present. Then changes begin. The pink becomes more intense, more vivid. Textures grow more pronounced. I see the tiny pores and fissures in the paintwork. I notice a little tingling of excitement in my chest. "This is nice," I say silently. I'm chattering again. And so it goes on.

Like any skill, meditation requires practice, lots of practice. The important thing is not to give up. With practice, the silences get longer and the effects filter down into daily life. But we can notice some effects almost immediately. The vision changes I've just experienced, for example. This isn't an optical distortion or a trance state. It's simple, old-fashioned expanded awareness freed from the filter of mind chatter. Becoming aware of our thoughts is the first step to silencing them. Once we go beyond the wall of words into inner silence, however briefly, we are in the present moment. As we notice without analyzing, interpreting, or judging, our perception is heightened and refined. We see with new eyes because we are free to be fully present, to experience whatever is before us right now—in my case, a pink wall.

EXERCISE 4: MEDITATION TO
SILENCE THE CHATTER

Preparation: Find a place to be alone and uninterrupted. Sit comfortably on a chair, on a cushion, or on the ground. Position yourself in such a way that your spine is erect and supported. You should feel relaxed but alert. This is a good position for all of the meditations in this book. You can do this meditation with your eyes closed or open, but if you choose open eyes, have an object such as a candle to focus on. If you are not accustomed to meditating, you might want to set a gentle-sounding alarm on your phone or a clock for ten minutes. You don't have to stop when the alarm sounds, but ten minutes is a good length of time for someone who is not used to meditation. If you are an experienced meditator, you may want to go longer than ten minutes or not set a timer at all. Breathe through your nose unless your nose is constricted.

Body Scan: Begin scanning your body by noticing your feet. How do your feet feel inside your shoes, or if you're not wearing shoes and socks, how does the air feel on the skin of your feet? Then move to your calves, thighs, buttocks, stom-ach. Notice everything—the contact with your clothing, the contact with the chair or floor, the temperature of the air. Look particularly for points of tension, and when you find them, consciously relax your muscles. Move your attention to your back, your stomach, your shoulders. Scan your arms and hands. Move on to your neck, a place where we hold a lot of tension, then your jaw, tongue, forehead, and scalp. A body scan is a good preliminary to the meditation and breathwork exercises throughout this book.

Meditation: When you have completed your body scan, focus your attention on your breathing. Don't change your breathing pattern; just pay attention to it. Be aware of the stages of inhale and exhale. Follow your breath into and out of your lungs. Keep breathing in this manner until you feel the pleasure of air entering your lungs. If your mind wanders, bring it back to your breathing.

When you are comfortable following your breathing, bring your attention to the point above your upper lip and below your nose, between your nostrils. Feel the cool air of inhale crossing this small point. Feel the warm air of exhale on the skin under your nose. If your mind wanders, bring it back to this point. Continue in this way until your alarm sounds.

When you finish meditating, take a few deep breaths, open your eyes if you had closed them, and begin to scan your body again. Notice the points of tension. Then, if you wish, make notes on your experience. Some people find it useful to write about their meditations in a journal. You have just spent at least part of the last ten minutes living in the present mo-ment. If you would like to experience the rejuvenating and calming effect meditation can have on both mind and body, meditate daily.

SCARY FREEDOM, SCARY INTIMACY

Silencing the mind is not necessarily easy, but it is a simple case of subtraction. When we take away the past and the future, we fall into the present moment in inner silence. With practice, we can prolong those seconds of silence. Eventually, we learn to live in the here and now. But initially, living in the present can feel uncomfortable. This is because all our Small Self defenses can be activated at the prospect of inner silence. To understand this more clearly, let's look at what goes on behind the scenes of an ordinary conversation at a party.

We meet someone new. They're talking. We look like we're listening. Part of us really is listening. But chances are, another part of us is racing ahead of the conversation, anticipating what they will say next and formulating our own response. At the same time, we're wondering, Do they like us? Do we like them? Where is this encounter going? If we do like them, we naturally put our best face forward. But our best face is not necessarily our real face. Sometimes we laugh at jokes that aren't funny, and sometimes we give an impression of ourselves that we know isn't quite the full picture.

Richard Rohr's book on mysticism is called *The Naked Now*, an inspired title. When we move into the present moment, we denude ourselves of everything that is familiar—our analyses, our store of knowledge, our interpretations and anticipations, our roles and image. When we stop analyzing the past, we stop protecting ourselves against it. When we stop anticipating the future, we stop buttressing ourselves against what might lie ahead. We face the unknown, and "anyone who stands on the edge of the unknown, fully in the present without reference point, experiences groundlessness."[13] Our protective wall of words is gone. We're naked, and nakedness makes most people feel vulnerable. When we are vulnerable, we are open. Openness is where transformation happens. This makes the now one of our greatest resources in dealing with both the past and the future. But until we learn to trust (the third practice), the now will also feel risky.

How would it feel if we were to be with the person at the party in the present moment, no jumping forward, no calculated responses? For many people, the prospect of such an unguarded encounter gives rise to a sense of unease, even risk. In the present moment we risk being seen as we are by another human being. We risk intimacy. Most people respond well to openness in another. Knowing people respond well to openness doesn't stop us from being afraid that if we ourselves are stripped of our Small Self defenses, they won't like us. So in the now, we also risk rejection. It can help us take that risk if we recognize that the now is also one of the safest places we can be.

The Safety of Now

Twenty years after the event, my client Marie told me about an early date with her ex-husband. He had just started a new job. It was the night of his company Christmas party, and he desperately wanted to make a good impression. But his car battery had died, and before he left home to pick up Marie, the car had to be jump-started. As a result, he was half an hour behind schedule arriving at her house. Marie lived a few miles in the opposite direction from the party venue, so they were definitely going to be late.

"He was irritated when he arrived," she told me. "You know, fidgety, dancing from one foot to the other while I got my coat. He started in on me in the car, telling me if I had been ready when he arrived, we wouldn't be late. I was ready. All I had to do was put on my coat, but it was all my fault. He was still going on about it when we pulled up to the party at the hotel.

"I opened the car door, and then I had this moment. I don't know what it was. The hotel, everything, seemed unreal. Sounds like something out of *Star Trek*, but time stopped. I was in a panic in the car the way he was going on at me. All that went away. I was just there. Right there. Calm. I knew what I should do. I knew I should find a taxi cab and go home and never see him again. But I didn't. It passed. I went to the party. Then I married him."

This one decades-old incident filled several therapy sessions. For many reasons that emerged during therapy, Marie grew up with an intense fear of never having a long-term relationship. The panic that she struggled with in the car had nothing to do with physical danger. A few years later, her husband punched her in the stomach, the first of many beatings. But that December night, Marie's greatest fear was that he would leave her.

Living in the present doesn't mean we don't think about the past or the future. We can learn from the past, and, in our society, we need to do some planning for the future. Living most of our lives in the past or the future is different from reviewing and planning. When we live mostly outside the present, there's usually some sort of Small Self emotional involvement. In Marie's case, fear tied her to the future. Her moment, as she called it, was a few seconds of complete presence in the now and complete connection with Big Self awareness. Fear of a future alone disappeared. She saw clearly what she needed to do. She just didn't do it. Being in the present brings that kind of clarity. The present shows us reality, and facing reality is usually a lot safer than following our illusions.

When we make real, present-moment connections with others, or, in Marie's case, with herself, it's surprising what opens up. As one of my favorite authors, Daniel O'Leary, puts it, "We will dance our way into amazing adventures."[14] We can't tell in advance what that adventure will be. We'll never know what turn Marie's life might have taken had she called a cab at the hotel that night. In the present, we don't know what the next moment will bring until it arrives. This is where the third key, trust and openness, comes into play.

EXERCISE 5: ANCHORING MEDITATION:
AN EXERCISE IN BEING PRESENT

Find a place where you won't be interrupted. Seat yourself comfortably in a chair that allows your spine to be erect and supported. Close your eyes and bring your attention to your breathing, following it in and out for about ten breaths. Focus your attention on the point of contact between your buttocks and the chair. Visualize your breath going right down into your buttocks and the area of your lower back and abdomen. Keep breathing slowly into this area, and at the same time, feel yourself heavily anchored to the chair. You are rooted in that spot. Breathe and feel the weight of your body rooting itself. Feel your spine stretch upward from this heavy, solid base.

When you feel strong in this position, open your eyes and look around. Notice what is before you, but don't follow it with your mind. This means you don't make any mental commentary on what you see. Just notice it and be present. Be aware of the core of your body and particularly your abdomen and lower spine. Look around as much as you like, slowly taking in the room but remaining anchored in your own body. This is what it feels like to be present.

EXERCISE 6: PRESENCE IN ACTION

Find a place where you won't be interrupted, and have a pen and notepad ready. Recall a conversation you had recently that was slightly contentious for you. Choose something that was not too emotionally charged—getting your child to tidy up after himself, for example. Run through the conversation in your mind just to get the outline of what happened, who said what, etc. These are the little events that made up the conversation. Write them down in your notepad. Here's an example:

> **Conversation:** *Telling my son he needs to clean up after himself in the kitchen.*
>
> **What happened:**
> 1. I asked him to give me a few minutes to talk.
> 2. I told him he left the kitchen in a mess the night before.
> 3. He rolled his eyes and started playing with his phone.
> 4. I told him to listen to me.
> 5. He sighed and put his phone down.
> 6. I told him he had to clean up after himself and that I couldn't clean up after him all the time.
> 7. He said his sister never has to clean up after herself and wanted to know why I treat her differently.
> 8. I told him I don't treat her differently and she always cleans up after she uses the kitchen.
> 9. He said "whatever" and walked away.

Now write the main points of your conversation on your notepad. When you've finished your review of the conversation, practice the anchoring meditation (exercise 5). When you feel solid and rooted in your center, return to normal breathing. Run through the conversation again, more slowly, this time focusing your own feelings at each stage of the encounter. Write down the feelings that passed through you at the time and why. Here's an example:

> **Conversation:** *Telling my son he needs to clean up after himself in the kitchen.*
>
> **My feelings and thoughts:**
> *Afraid because I knew what was coming.*
> *Afraid because I know he can be cutting.*
> *Angry—this happens all the time.*
> *I wanted to slap him—he has no respect for me.*
> *Guilty—maybe he's right, maybe I'm not a good parent.*
> *Frustrated, disappointed because I lost again.*

Review your list of emotional reactions and thoughts, then ask yourself, "How many of those feelings were generated either by my remembering past experiences or anticipating future outcomes?" If you look at the sample list in the example, the emotions were generated by remembering previous conversations and by anticipating that the current conversation would have the same outcome.

Now imagine you have no history with the person in question. You have known them for no longer than a day. Because you have nothing to look back on, you have nothing to base fears of the future on. You are rooted in the present moment, fully present to the conversation. How would that change your feelings? In the previous example of the parent trying to get her son to clean the kitchen, the parent would likely not have felt any fear because she would not have anticipated a negative outcome. She certainly wouldn't have bought into guilt, and her anger would have been a fraction of what she actually did feel.

Feelings drive our actions and responses. If you did not have to contend with the feelings generated by remembering the past and anticipating the future, would your behavior have been different? In chapter 7, we will return in detail to the question of how we shape our own world. Right now, just take each of the feelings you listed and ask yourself: "If I hadn't felt _____, how would I have reacted?"

Our conversations, our actions and reactions, are usually more effective if they are not mired in the past or designed to effect some anticipated outcome. The second practice, Living in the Present, is pertinent to every one of the issues we will examine in part 2 of this book. Although the second practice is not specifically called out in each chapter, the present moment offers us the transformational balm of peace and stillness in every life situation. Free from the burden of both past and future, awareness blossoms and oneness beckons. But for us to be able to leave the past behind us and the future in the unknown, we need to pay attention to the third practice: Trust and Openness.

TRUST AND OPENNESS

During her "moment" in the hotel parking lot, Marie saw her future husband for who he was. But she didn't trust herself to manage her own future. Instead, her needs and fears kicked in and she ignored what she had seen. The result: nearly fifteen years of abuse.

Marie spent her first six months in therapy trying to answer one question: Why me? I have spent many hours with clients who were abused as children, listening to them ask that same question over and over again. I can give them all the standard information about abusers grooming children who are in some way vulnerable, but it takes a long time for them to stop searching for the reason they personally were singled out. It is similar for people like Marie, who have been abused or betrayed in adult relationships or let down by friends or colleagues. Their world was turned upside down by the betrayal. If they could only find the reason for the behavior, the logic behind what the other person did, then they could make the world right again and life could go on as before.

It's hard to find a satisfactory answer to "Why me?" We may never know what was going on in the other person's mind. But on the road to recovery, the question has to be explored. It has to be explored in part because of the light it sheds on the issue of trust.

We tend to think of trust in terms of other people. We trust. We expect follow-through. They don't deliver. It was perfectly reasonable for Marie to expect the man who publicly declared his love for her in marriage to respect her. It's perfectly reasonable for children to expect adults will keep them safe. It's reasonable for all of us to expect colleagues to stick to project deadlines and friends to refrain from having affairs with our partners. But people don't always deliver, and sometimes we let them down too. The kind of trust that involves expectations is wide open to betrayal, and the pain involved can be excruciating.

But spiritual trust has nothing to do with other people. Spiritual trust is a way of being. We trust in life itself, and we trust our own Big

Self. If you feel betrayed or let down by somebody, the road from expectation-based trust to spiritual trust, where betrayal is not an issue, goes through several stages.

STAGES ON THE ROAD TO TRUST

Anger: Marie had accumulated a large store of anger toward her ex-husband and an equally wide range of expletives to describe him. Depending on the depth of the betrayal, it's natural to feel anything from irritation to rage. We blame and demonize and fantasize about revenge. Sometimes people need justice in the form of a prosecution or some other official punishment. Others need privacy. And somewhere in the mix there's usually a substantial dose of self-blame.

Self-Blame: Children in particular desperately need to believe there is order in the universe. Adults don't just abuse or leave or die. There must be a reason. So they take responsibility themselves, blame themselves. Marie tortured herself about what she could have done differently, how she could have been a better wife or lover. Maybe that would have made the marriage work. It's a stage people have to go through and get beyond because the next stage is crucial to developing spiritual trust.

Responsibility: Marie's "moment" was one of awakening to reality, radical awareness. She saw her future husband for who he was at that time. Twenty years later, she recognized the moment as a warning sign. Sometimes there aren't just warning signs; there are screeching alarms, flashing lights, and a sea of red flags. Other people can see them, but we can't. We are not responsible for another person's actions. We don't "make" them betray our trust, but we are responsible for our own recovery. Nobody else can do it for us. Part of that recovery means examining the role we played in being hurt by the betrayal.

We play a role in our own hurt by:

- **Ignoring signs:** Because we want something so much, we often shut down our awareness, blinding ourselves to the reality before us. I once worked for a small charity where I could see the fault lines my first week on the job. I wanted so much to believe in the goodness of this organization that I ignored the signs. I even argued with people who criticized it. A year later, I had to face the flaws other people had acknowledged from the beginning. Marie so desperately wanted a happily-ever-after marriage that she ignored her husband's habit of blaming her for things he did himself. A week before her wedding, her father, his eyes unblinkered by need, asked her not to go through with the marriage. She chose to proceed with her plans.

- **Accepting poor treatment:** This can begin with very small things we ignore because we don't want to create a fuss, stand up to someone, or take a risk. In this way, we open the door to a pattern of relationship where we are treated with less than respect.

- **Falling into coping behavior patterns:** Instead of taking a stand early in a relationship, we develop ways of coping with the unsatisfactory situation. A woman I worked with many years ago never met deadlines. Never. She got away with it because none of her colleagues, me included, took a stand on the issue. We endured it, covered up for it, turned it into a joke. When we're afraid to stand up for ourselves, our relationship soon falls into a pattern, a dance between two people that's hard to change. It's almost as if we give them permission to treat us with less than respect. Betrayal of trust may not be far behind.

EXERCISE 7: IGNORING SIGNS

You'll need a paper and pen for this exercise. Divide your page
into two columns. Put the heading "The Signs" at the top of
the left-hand column and "My Reactions" at the top on the
right. Choose a relationship that you feel is not as respectful
or problem-free as you would like it to be. Begin with a relationship that is not too emotionally charged—a neighbor or
acquaintance, for example. You can move to more emotionally difficult relationships later. Review the early months of
that relationship. Were there any red flags, any warning signs
of trouble to come? If so, what was your reaction to those
signs? Here's an example:

The Relationship: *A friend I made while working together on a committee. We were great friends, but suddenly he began picking fights with me and now barely speaks to me.*	
THE SIGNS	MY REACTIONS
He had conflicts with other people.	*I ignored it because he didn't fight with me. Because he confided in me, I thought we would never end up fighting.*
He talked to me about other people and how wrong and stupid they were.	*I felt flattered that he trusted me and thought I was special and different.*

We ignore signs and accept poor treatment for reasons
that lie deep within us. Uncovering and facing those reasons
can be painful, and the process demands a high level of honesty with ourselves. People who follow this process to completion can eventually break through to a new life. Those who
are able to look at their own responsibility—their blindness

to signs, their acceptance of poor treatment or even abuse, their own adaptations and self-deceptions—these are the ones who grow from what they once saw as betrayal. For those abused as children, this may mean accepting the fact that they did nothing to cause the abuse.

In the future, their eyes will be open wider, but not in a furtive, fearful, searching-for-signs way. They are more open to life and the risk involved in living than ever before. Paradoxically, because they are more awake to what is, they will be less likely to end up in another serious betrayal than people who live in a cocoon of caution. This is not because they see others more clearly. Rather, it's because they see themselves more clearly and honestly. Once Marie figured out why she so desperately wanted to be married, the need to be in a relationship lost its grip on her. The ghost of that need resurfaced from time to time, and she recognized it as her Achilles' heel. She went on to date other men. There were more signs. She heeded the warnings.

In the ground of honesty and self-responsibility, spiritual trust grows. Future betrayals, if they occur, are more likely to elicit healthy feelings of anger and disappointment rather than gut-wrenching devastation. One of the reasons: when acting out of radical awareness, we have far fewer expectations of others. If our eyes are open, we will know that sometimes other people do let us down. Spiritual trust is not trust in someone or something. Rather, trust is the matrix in which we move. If I trust myself and life, I will know that whatever happens, it is part of life, part of what is, and I will be able to deal with and grow from it. Trust is no longer "trust in." It's simply trust. A state of being.

With trust, we can be open to the full experience of life, to the path we cannot yet see, to the wisdom we do not yet have, to the transformation we cannot envision because we are not there yet. Every single thing that happens to us is grist for the mill of life. Everything has a place in our lives because, if we are open to it, we can grow from it. Trust does not mean there will be no more suffering. Instead, trust offers us the tools we need to grow out of suffering and to turn pain into new life. Trust and openness empower us to grow from the most difficult times and the most painful experiences. It makes the fourth practice, Growing from Adversity, possible.

Without trust, we will be too fearful to stay open. We will be so busy trying to control the next moment that we will miss the present one. Daniel O'Leary writes: "It is only when we take the leap of faith with abandonment that the wind blows fair to fill our sails ... It is an aching, breaking, ecstatic, valley-low, mountain-high adventure."[15]

5

THE FOURTH AND FIFTH PRACTICES:

Growing from Adversity into Oneness

It's a shallow life that doesn't give a person a few scars.
~GARRISON KEILLOR, *A PRAIRIE HOME COMPANION*

I once served on the management team of an after-school program for young children from under-resourced neighborhoods. A statistical profile of this group of children anywhere in the Western world would predict that the majority of them would drop out of school early. This alone would condemn them to a lifetime of minimum-wage poverty. Some would serve time in prison, others in treatment centers. To help the children keep up with grade level, the one-to-one instructors patiently showed them how to shape their letters—A, B, C.

Over the past few decades, research on emotional intelligence has blossomed. That research shows that a key element in success—no matter how you define it—is the ability to defer gratification, the ability to sacrifice short-term gain for greater rewards in the future. Deferring gratification hinges on the ability to tolerate pain—in this case, frustration.

The instructors used chalkboards. If a child made a mistake with a letter, all they had to do was erase it and start again. The future of those children in the after-school program could be read not in their level of intelligence but in their reaction to failure. The children who could tolerate the frustration of failure erased their mistakes and began again. These children learned their letters. The little boys and girls who needed immediate success and threw tantrums when they failed to form perfect letters learned at a much slower pace. Because they had not learned to endure the pain of embarrassment and frustration, they were destined to fall further and further behind in school.

In his beautiful book *Care of the Soul*, writer and therapist Thomas Moore writes: "The soul presents itself in a variety of colors, including all the shades of gray, blue and black. To care for the soul, we must observe the full range of all its colorings, and resist the temptation to approve only of ... the brilliant colors."[16] Every major spiritual tradition has its own way of telling us that life is made up of both light and dark and that the dark is as valuable as the light. Eastern traditions speak of yin and yang—everything eventually flows into its opposite. Christianity has the Paschal mystery—death becomes resurrection. Poets speak of the darkness before the dawn, the dark night of the soul. In our lives, we all have periods of joy and contentment and we have periods of suffering.

Sigmund Freud, the father of modern psychotherapy, offered a more psychological explanation for the role of pain in our lives. According to Freud, we have a natural impetus to seek pleasure: the pleasure principle. Pain, when it's great enough, moves us to action, moves us to make the changes we need to achieve pleasure. The dark time, the pain, is the engine of growth. Whatever the symbol or metaphor we use, they all illustrate the basic paradox of life: suffering exists, but out of it can come even greater life, because, as Pema Chödrön writes, "to stay with that shakiness—to stay with a broken heart, with a rumbling stomach, with the feeling of hopelessness and wanting to get revenge—that is the path of true awakening."[17]

A cornerstone of Buddhist philosophy on suffering is that it is caused by desire. We want. We don't get. We suffer as a result. Eliminate desire and you eliminate suffering. One of the key features of the oneness state is satiation. We desire nothing other than to be in that moment. In his book *The Power of Now*, Eckhart Tolle describes a oneness state that lasted for two years. During that time, he felt no suffering because he felt no desire. Most of us are not there yet, but the contemplative mind, the mind we develop through spiritual experience, teaches us that a vital step along the way is to learn to be present to suffering. Because regardless of how we frame it, the deepest, most profound transformation seems to come through suffering.

I've had many occasions to be grateful to the pharmaceutical industry for creating painkillers and have encouraged several clients to consult their doctor about taking antidepressants. But when we rush to medicate emotional pain, we run the risk of missing the life-transforming power of the dark times. Our society does not do a great job of teaching people how to live with pain. In addition to prescribed drugs, we have developed many ways to medicate away emotional pain. They include:

- **Addiction:** Alcohol, drugs, eating, not eating, work, sex, etc.
- **Behavior patterns:** Giving in, rebelling, playing helpless, taking charge, whatever has worked in the past.
- **Avoidance:** Flitting from one relationship to another or one job to another, compulsive socializing or avoiding social contact as much as possible, etc.
- **Denial:** Pushing the pain or the situation that generates pain out of our conscious awareness. If all else fails, old-fashioned denial can keep pain at bay for long periods of time.

The chronic avoidance of emotional pain often brings greater long-term suffering. Addictions that develop to help us cope end up adding to our pain and make life miserable for the people who love us. In difficult relationships, denying our own needs and preferences is a dubious insurance policy against being left alone. Denying our needs in a relationship in order to avoid conflict sets up an unhealthy dynamic that can destroy the relationship instead of nurturing it. Paradoxically, we can end up alone anyway. The contemplative mind teaches us that there is a different way.

ALCHEMY

When things are going well and life is good, it's natural to want it to stay that way. Then something happens. It could be something minor, one of the small ups and downs we encounter every day that seem so important at the time. Or it could be a major life event. The kids grow up and leave home. Someone dies. A relationship or marriage ends. We lose our job or are hit by illness or depression. It seems like a terrible thing, and sometimes the pain is so great, we don't want to live.

Suffering leads us into liminal space, the space is where our normal way of doing things no longer works and nothing is as it was.

Richard Rohr writes, "Some native peoples call liminal space 'crazy time.' It's time where nothing looks like what we're used to, like the time after the death of someone you love."[18]

In liminal space, we metaphorically throw our hands up and admit we don't know where to go next. This is surrender. We surrender to life, to our Big Self, to not knowing. When we are fully present to our own pain in trust and surrender, then we begin to see with new eyes. We begin to see with a beginner's mind.

The beginner's mind allows the Paschal mystery to occur. The miracle of alchemy transforms death into new life. Rohr says, "The old world is able to fall apart and the new world is able to be revealed."[19] We discover new ways forward that we couldn't possibly have conjured up through our old ways of thinking and coping. Then, as Daniel O'Leary writes, "a blessed peace, a greater understanding and a deeper insight into the meaning within the dark feelings is released within us—revealing the way through, into the growing, loving spaces of our liberated souls."[20]

When we embrace the terror of being alone, divorce can open up a whole new life. In the emptiness of a home where children have grown up and moved on, we can find a new and deeper meaning for our existence. When we face adversity and loss full on, we can discover depths and strengths we never knew were within us. As Japanese poet Masahide put it, "Barn's burnt down. Now I can see the moon."

When we're in the midst of pain and struggle, it can be difficult, often impossible, to see that any good could come of such suffering. The skill of growing from adversity lies in holding the discomfort within us with trust and openness even though the solution is nowhere in sight. The old word for this is faith. Faith is knowing (not believing, but knowing) that, in Julian of Norwich's famous words, "All shall be well ..." Knowing, trusting, that all will be well is what carries us through the darkness into new life. Here is an exercise to help you find the learning from the hard times in your own life.

EXERCISE 8: FINDING THE LEARNING

Take time to recall a few of the more difficult experiences in your life. Choose one or two. Then ask yourself, "How did I grow as a result of that event? What did I learn from it?" Write down some of your thoughts. If your immediate response is "nothing," put that aside for now and dig deeper. Sometimes it helps to rephrase the questions as, "If I were to have learned something from this experience, what would it be?" Your response may be that no matter what you learned, it wasn't worth the pain. In this case, mastering the five practices and developing a contemplative mind will help make the next dark time both easier and more transformational. If your experience of suffering made you close down and become bitter or angry, please take the time to really work the five practices, preferably with the support of a therapist or support group.

EXERCISE 9: BE YOUR OWN WITNESS

Find a comfortable spot where you won't be interrupted. Review your life as it is right now. Is there anything happening that is a source of emotional suffering for you? Choose something that's not too difficult. You can progress to more highly charged situations later.

Practice the anchoring meditation (exercise 5) from chapter 4 to root yourself in your body. When you feel anchored in the present, allow your breathing to come to its natural pace and depth, but keep it rhythmic, with no pauses in the cycle of inhale and exhale. Then in your own time, review the situation that's causing you pain from the Witness position. Be a detached witness looking in on your own life. Watch yourself play out a scenario as if you were an actor in a movie.

That character in the movie, the one who looks and sounds like you, what could he or she learn in this situation? As a detached witness, you're not blinded by emotion, by suffering, by getting caught up in the situation. As a detached witness, you have a long-term, clear-sighted perspective. If you find yourself slipping into the movie inside your head, bring your awareness back to your breathing. Keep observing until you see the learning, the potential for growth, in the situation. What suggestions would you make to the character in the movie?

Here's an example:

The Situation: *I'm completely drained by the bad atmosphere at work, where everyone gossips about everyone else. My colleagues come to me every day to talk about each other. They take up my time, so I'm falling behind in my work. It's getting to the point that I hate going to work. I can't do anything because I'm friends with them and people need to vent. I feel I'm stuck and just have to put up with the situation.*

Potential for Growth:
- *I could develop the skills to say no graciously, or at least limit the time I spend listening.*
- *I could practice breathing and meditation in the moment so I can listen without being drained.*
- *I could explore what it is about me that attracts gossip into my life. Do I have weak boundaries? Do I encourage gossip or contribute to it in any way? Do I prompt people to say more without realizing that's what I'm doing?*
- *I know chronic gossip can be the result of problems in the organization's culture. Can I help solve those problems in any way?*

The hard times, the periods of suffering we all go through, are some of the most spiritually fertile times of our lives. St. John of the Cross wrote about the "dark night of the soul." The Bible tells the story of Jonah's sojourn in the belly of the whale, while Job endured a veritable marathon of suffering. But if we can open ourselves to adversity, however great or small our problems might be, we open ourselves to the fifth practice: Oneness.

THE FIFTH PRACTICE: ONENESS

An infant cannot distinguish between himself and the objects in his universe. When you take the bright, noisy toy away, he doesn't try to look for it. This is because once you take the object out of his field of vision, it ceases to exist for him. He and his universe are one, and he cannot conceive of a state in which there is a subject and an object, a you and a me, a state that is not unitive—a state that is not oneness. You know the baby has reached the point of separating himself from everything else in his world when he starts to look for the toy that has just disappeared. The toy now has a separate existence of its own. He and the toy are no longer one. They are two, and we have duality. From this early separation, we build a worldview based on dualism. Awareness of duality is vital for navigating life. Dualistic thinking, the ability to hold a phenomenon before us and objectively examine it, is invaluable. It enables us to evaluate, learn, and shape the world in which we live. It is an engine of technological and economic progress. But if we sink too deeply into dualistic thinking, it can become a major barrier to full-on engagement with life.

Dualism is the dominant mode of thinking in Western society, the dominant way of seeing and interpreting the world. It permeates our culture, our education systems, health care, politics, advertising, the way we categorize experience. Dualism is so integral to the way we describe the world to ourselves that it's difficult to see in the details of daily life. It comes more into focus if we pull back to a bird's-eye view and from there work our way down to the life of each person.

THE WORLD OUT THERE

In his book *The Audacity of Hope*, Barack Obama skillfully describes the depth of dualistic thinking in American politics. After the Reagan presidency, "the lines were drawn in more sharply ideological terms … You were for either tax cuts or tax hikes, small government or big government … you either supported unchecked development, drilling, strip-mining … or you supported stifling bureaucracy and red tape that choked off growth."[21] The divisions may be less delineated in other countries, but most political parties have a core of loyal supporters who do not cross party lines, no matter what. They either fail to see or refuse to support what is good in the other party's platform. This is dualistic thinking written large.

It's often difficult to see the connection between politicians making decisions in a faraway government and the ordinary man or woman working in an office or factory. But there *is* a direct connection. Political decisions do trickle down into the lives of ordinary people. The economic pie is cut according to those decisions, whether we recognize that or not. We all live with the effects of dualism.

THE WORLD RIGHT HERE

Dualistic thinking is not confined to the distant stage of national politics or foreign policy. Closer to home, I have worked on the edges of community activism for many years. Community development workers serve the most vulnerable and marginalized people in society. Yet getting caught up in ideology and the defense of entrenched positions is as much an occupational hazard for local community idealists as it is for national politicians.

Community-based youth programs and mainstream schools, for example, often have great difficulty working together, each criticizing the other for the problems they are both dedicated to solving. The result of this divide affects the lives of the often needy children they both serve. This is "them and us" thinking. Soon mythologies grow up around "them": they don't care, they want everything for themselves, they aren't interested in the good of everyone. Myths take on the solidity of truth, and camps become more and more entrenched. Dualistic splits affect even the small details of our daily lives.

We divide life into categories and assign hierarchies of value to them. Some things are good, others bad, some are right or wrong, valuable or not valuable. In our popular culture, being thin is good and plump is bad. Young is good and old is bad. One particular fashion is acceptable and another is not. The media trade on this dualistic approach to life, pronouncing some artists acceptable, cool, and edgy and others passé.

Harmless? Not for the elderly person who has become invisible in a whole range of social situations, not for the overweight teenager who agonizes about her size every day, not for the struggling musician who produces great music but is ignored by the music industry.

The dualistic approach is at the heart of much that is painful and tragic in the world. When we make something or someone less important, less valuable, less acceptable, we risk creating great pain for ourselves and others. My country is right and yours is wrong. My god is right and yours is wrong. My race, color, gender, tribe, class, accent, shape, or size is right and yours is wrong. These are the divisions by which bullying, racism, and cruelty are justified every day in small and not-so-small ways.

Even if we are on the apparently winning side, we still pay a price. Many years ago I taught in a Catholic girls' school. One day a nun visited the school and spoke to the assembled student body. I cannot remember anything about her or why she was there. What I do remember was her telling us that God loves everyone but particularly favors Catholics. It's not a statement you hear much from Catholics anymore. Perhaps it's difficult to sustain such arrogance when the dark side of the church has been so spectacularly exposed. With that one statement about God favoring Catholics, that one split in the field of her perception, the nun not only alienated the three Muslim students in my English class, but she shut herself off from the richness and wonder of all other religions. Here is what Joan Chittister, another Catholic nun, has to say about this kind of narrowness: "There are few things in life more threatening to the person whose religion is parochialism than the alien and few things more revelatory to the contemplative than the stranger."[22] Dualistic thinking shrinks our world to the point where we miss out on the abundance life has to offer.

THE WORLD IN ME

Dualism is not just "out there" in the world; it's within us. It shows itself in our way of thinking and relating. The friendship between Gillian, a former client of mine, and her friend Mary illustrates the damage dualistic thinking can cause in the lives of ordinary people.

Friendship blossomed quickly when Gillian got a job in the company where Mary worked. In the middle of a particularly dreary winter, they planned and booked a two-week vacation to North Africa together. A month before they were due to leave for Tripoli, Mary pulled out of the trip. Her only explanation was, "I don't want to go." Gillian was shocked, puzzled, and then, understandably, angry.

Anger is a natural response to hurt. It gets us past the early stages when the pain is sharpest. Then it subsides—unless it's fed by dualistic thinking. That's exactly what happened to Gillian. She began to review her relationship with Mary. Small things previously overlooked leaped out at her. Mary sometimes didn't call when she said she would. Mary once canceled a dinner arrangement at the last minute. Mary promised to join a sailing club with Gillian, then changed her mind. Friends and family joined in, trying to be helpful. A head of steam built up. Soon Mary became "a bitch" that Gillian was "better off without." For Gillian and her other friends, Mary lost some of her humanity. This happens with dualistic thinking. We turn people into "them." "They" are different from us, wrong, subtly inferior.

This pattern of dehumanizing others plays out many times a day in small ways. Ask any parking enforcement officer how often they get yelled at for ticketing cars, even though the driver knowingly parked illegally. Students often objectify their teachers. I know I did. It makes teachers fair game in the classroom. Teachers sometimes do the same thing with their students, losing sight of the humanity of the "problem" child who causes them so much heartache. At home, even if only in our own minds, we can blame our children or our parents or our partner for what we see as being wrong in our family. And herein lies the block to spiritual growth. As long as we focus on "them," we don't have to look at "us," and awareness of "us" is the starting point of spiritual and personal growth.

There's often a hook to hang this hat of blame upon. Mary let Gillian down badly. But years after their friendship ended, Gillian found out that Mary had been in an abusive relationship at the time of their quarrel. Her boyfriend would not let her go on vacation without him. Like many women in that situation, Mary kept the abuse a secret. But the dualistic mental process Gillian went through at the time kept her from asking the questions that would have explained Mary's actions. It cost them both a friendship.

The more we make the other person wrong, the more our own life contracts. We sacrifice the precious opportunity to grow, to expand, to embrace new life through encountering other people and other experiences. This is a lot to sacrifice on the cross of duality. There is wisdom in loving our enemies.

The Wider View—Oneness

The essence of mystical experience is nonduality, or oneness. All boundaries of time and space, all concepts and barriers that separate us from anything other than us, fall away. Opposites come together in something that is greater than the two alone. As William Blake put it in his poem "Auguries of Innocence," in a state of oneness you can "see a world in a grain of sand / And a heaven in a wild flower / Hold infinity in the palm of your hand / And eternity in an hour."

This is not a fuzzy merging with another. It's not as if I have a mystical experience in which you and I become one. You are still you and I am still me, but we are one in something that's more than both of us, in the matrix in which we exist, in the "ground of being." It's an expanded state of consciousness, a state of radical awareness that can never be adequately described in words. In it, we become aware of the unifying principle that lies behind all apparent divisions. For many people, this naturally gives rise to the question "Oneness with what?"

GODS AND RELIGIONS

The most important book I've ever read was written by a Catholic priest. *Travelling Light* by Daniel O'Leary got me through one of the darkest times in my life. The book is full to overflowing with warmth, wisdom, hope, and love—and references to the Christian God. As someone who no longer classifies herself as Christian, I could have easily dismissed the book without reading it, and what a loss that would have been! Likewise, a devout Christian or Muslim might dismiss the books of someone like Ken Wilber because they are too secular. That, too, would be a great loss to the reader. So many people have been turned off to spirituality by their experience of organized religion that their concept of God gets in the way of the freedom to embrace what can be one of the most precious parts of life—their own spirituality. This is true as much for those who have embraced evangelical religions as it is for those with an aversion to all things religious. Because of these differences, it's important to explore briefly the topics of religion and God.

Religion is a concept, a structure, a set of theological tenets, a building, a community, a set of practices, rules, and behaviors. Many people are turned off by the language of religion—sin, conversion, salvation.

But in keeping with the endless paradoxes of the spiritual life, religion and spirituality can be the same thing *and* can be totally different. Religion is what develops over time among a group of people who share a spiritual experience or whose ancestors once shared that experience. Strip away the organization, the dogma and rules, dig deep into the past, and you will find the spiritual heart of most religions. Spirituality is difficult to define precisely because it is an experience. Words like "union" or "oneness" are vague terms, hard to pin down; they are so open to interpretation as to undermine their credibility. They beg to be made more tangible. Here is where we run into the concept of God.

Mystical states are generally characterized by feelings of connection with self, but also by a distinct perception that this self is part of something greater than what we normally think of as our "self." If our experience is nature-based, we can perceive a merging of ourselves and nature. Often mystical experience is a perception of oneness, not with anything or anyone, but of merging into a greater, vibrant, loving whole. It's not a huge step from there to extrapolate the existence of a life force that is separate from and greater than our little individual life. Etty Hillesum, an extraordinary young Dutch woman who died at Auschwitz concentration camp, explained the link between spirituality and God: "When I pray ... I hold a silly, naïve or deadly serious dialogue with what is deepest inside me, which, for the sake of convenience, I'll call God."[23]

I myself cannot use the word "God" to describe my spiritual experiences. It feels far too limiting. It conjures up images of Jesus, Krishna, Shiva, Pan, or any number of other names and faces people have given to deities over the centuries. For me, the name and shape immediately create separation because they give the impression that God is outside of us. Therefore, we must aspire to union with him, and it is usually a him. We have duality in place of oneness.

Visualizing this remarkably human-looking, omnipotent, and external God easily leads to the development of a set of theories about what God thinks and how he behaves. In time, these become doctrines, articles of faith, rules to be obeyed as the way to connect with God. A religion is born, a church develops. Unfortunately, our religion quite often becomes the one true religion, the only way to God, better than any other religion. The church can become more important than the spiritual experience it is supposed to be facilitating for its members. Eventually, the spiritual experience can be completely lost, buried beneath the weight of doctrine, moral laws, and codes of behavior. By no means do all religions follow this path, but a brief review of history tells us it's a common pattern.

This is a lot of baggage for any word to carry and one of the reasons I don't like to use the word "God." We're still left with the question "Union with what?" Eckhart Tolle calls it "Being." One of my closest friends calls it "Lucy." My answer has varied over the years. For now I call it "Life," but I leave it up to the readers to delve deeply into their own lived experience and answer the question for themselves. They may want to call it "God."

No matter how we answer the question "One with what?" for ourselves, in this state of oneness, everyone, even our enemy, is ultimately made of the same stuff. Here there is love. This is not a sentimental, needs-based love focused on an individual. This is an eyes-wide-open, fully awake love that is a state of being rather than something we give and receive. Daniel O'Leary says that in this state, we "cannot hate someone else and love ourselves any more than we can hate ourselves and love someone else."[24] The "them and us," black-and-white stance dissolves. There is a softening of attitude and heart.

Oneness is not about suspending moral or ethical discernment. In a state of spiritual love, we are less needy. When we don't need love or approval or patronage or favor from someone else, our vision clears. We're free to see and respond differently. We can see people more for who they are and less for who we want them to be. Love divested of need is both profoundly ethical and deeply compassionate. Relationships, like the friendship between Gillian and Mary, may never work out because it takes two to make any kind of relationship work. But when we approach life through the consciousness of oneness, we don't waste precious years wound up tight behind anger and hurt.

Nondualistic thinking also makes for a safer journey through life. We are more likely to see those red flags and hear the warning bells. And because we are more open, we resist the flow of life less. Therefore, as Ken Wilber writes, "there is nothing outside of [us] to smash into [us], bruise [us], torment [us]."[25] We can grow from the darkness, because in the long run, all will be well.

EXERCISE 10: FEELING LOVED

Do you ever feel unloved or separated in any way from the benevolence of life? If you do, take a few minutes to anchor yourself in the present using the anchoring meditation (exercise 5) from chapter 4. Breathe with awareness until you experience the physical pleasure of breathing. Then enjoy the sensation in your chest. Sink into it until you feel the contentment that breathing with awareness can bring. Let the words "I am loved" swim in your mind and your body. Keep breathing and say the words in rhythm with your breath. If breathing without words is more fulfilling for you, let the words fade but keep your awareness on that feeling of warm contentment in your chest. Keep breathing until you feel ready to finish this exercise.

EXERCISE 11: LOVE IN LIFE

You'll need a pen and paper for this exercise. Recall the feeling of contentment and love from exercise 10. A little inner voice may tell you that this idea of being loved and cherished by life, of being one with life, is silly, a figment of your imagination. Ask the voice to be quiet for now, and return to the feeling of contentment, of oneness with yourself. If you carried this feeling into your daily life, how would it affect the way you interact with others? How would it affect your level of optimism, the way you approach tasks, the way you face change? Write down your thoughts in response to the following question: "If I felt one with life, how would that feeling affect the way I live day today?"

PART 2
SPIRITUALITY IN ACTION

Carpe diem, quam minimum credula postero.
(Seize the day, trusting as little as possible in the future.)

~HORACE, ODES 1.11

INTRODUCTION TO PART 2

When we allow our experiences of oneness to transform our outlook, life opens up for us rather than closing in. When we are substantially free of fear, we can be open to people, ideas, and experiences we once rejected. How many things do we say no to in a day? I know people who will not even taste certain food, not because they've already tasted and disliked it but because they've decided in advance that they don't like it. Obviously it's wise to say no to some things, but how many times do we say no to simple things—types of music, food, clothes, etc.? These are the small things that make daily life richer. When we are open not just to new sensual experiences but to the foreigner, the person of a different color, the homeless person, the old, the young, the Catholic or Muslim, the religious fanatic or atheist, we ourselves are stretched and expanded in new ways and into new places. If we live in the world of them and us, black and white, we miss out on the richness hidden in all those shades of gray.

It's not always easy to see ourselves closing down. It's not always easy to understand how we ourselves stop life from grabbing hold of us and taking us on an adventure. We don't notice the small choices we make throughout any given day that keep life at bay. All we know is that we have arrived at a point of wanting more. The second half of this book is about the many ways in which we prevent ourselves from storming our heaven, from experiencing the rich texture of life on a daily basis, and about how the five practices can help us change this.

Each chapter in part 2 will cover one of the major obstacles to full engagement living, to oneness, that people face. We will examine each issue in detail, painting a picture in stories of how it operates in people's lives. When we understand what we're dealing with, when we recognize its shape and form, we will look at the role the five practices can play in turning our limitations into opportunities, our half-living into the wholehearted joy of oneness.

All five practices are relevant to the topic of each chapter, but some are more pertinent than others. Each chapter, therefore, will focus on the most important practice for that particular topic. The chapters will also contain exercises to help you put the practices into action in your own life. We will begin our exploration with a look at dynamic breathwork, one of the most effective practices I know for entering states of oneness.

6

EXPERIENCING ONENESS:
Breathwork and Other Techniques

Feelings come and go like clouds in a windy sky.
Conscious breathing is my anchor.
~THICH NHAT HANH, *STEPPING INTO FREEDOM*

One of the most popular techniques I use with groups is visualization. The majority of group members I've worked with love to be guided into a world inside their imagination. They love to be taken to beaches and meadows, to float on clouds and swim in underwater caverns, their personal safe place. As a group member, visualization leaves me cold. And techniques that rely on a degree of visualization, such as Time Line Therapy, have no effect on me. This doesn't mean the technique itself is ineffective. I have plenty of evidence that visualizations, like the ones used throughout this book, are extremely effective. It's just not the technique for me.

The spiritual technique or therapy that suits one person may leave another unmoved. What suits us at one stage in our development may not be effective at all at a later stage. In my experience, people are mysteriously drawn to what suits them. The technique, the therapy, seems to show up in their life at the right time. A smaller number of people dabble and search, often for years, before settling on anything. A word of caution: dabbling can be an excellent way to avoid commitment to the work of personal growth. No matter how amazing our routine, we don't attain fitness in one workout. And we don't reach nirvana in one meditation session. We need to commit to a technique or a therapy for several sessions before making the decision to move on.

If you are ready to find a therapy or spiritual technique, the information in this chapter can be the starting point in your search for the approach that best suits you. Because the bulk of my professional and personal experience lies in breathwork, and because I've found breathwork to be incredibly effective for a wide variety of people, I'm going to cover that technique in detail before progressing to an overview of therapy, meditation, and other techniques.

THE BREATHWORK EXPERIENCE

Bodies lie in random patterns across the wooden floor, one hundred twenty or so of them, more than twenty nationalities and I don't know how many languages.

"Follow your breath, deep into your body." The instructor's voice is sultry, accented. She weaves her way carefully around the people lying on the floor, maintaining an overview, while a team of assistants bend down here and there to whisper personalized instructions.

This is the opening day of the annual Global Inspiration Conference, a weeklong celebration of breathwork that takes place in a different country each year. It's the "group breathe" that invariably kicks off the conference. Most of the people lying on the floor are familiar with meditative breathing—the mindful following of the breath on its path into and out of the body. But when this instructor says "follow your breath," it's just the beginning of a dynamic inner journey. That journey will meander through layer upon layer of emotions, memories, life experiences. It will end about forty-five minutes later at the mystical, blissful state of oneness.

The breathers follow instructions, expanding their breathing with each inhale. Every one of them is aware of where they are and what they're doing, but one by one they surrender to their own breathing. You can see it. Chests expand and contract rhythmically, filling to capacity, exhaling fully like a complex choreographed dance where everyone moves independently yet somehow they all fit together. The breath takes on a life of its own. Then someone breaks the rhythm and begins to cry. Others follow. Assistants squat down to offer tissues or the delicious comfort of a hand resting on the forehead or shoulder. Someone else laughs, a deep belly laugh that permeates their whole body, a hilarious private joke. Still more remain perfectly calm, absorbed in their own inner universe. Then, as if some tipping point has been reached, tears dry up, emotions subside, and the room is bathed in an almost visible peace. The assistants move off to the side and sit together in groups, relaxed yet still attentive. The people on the floor stretch, turn on their side, and luxuriate in the blissful world their own breath has opened within them. The leader moves to the sound system and puts on something classical, and she too lounges on a pile of cushions. Later, when the breathers sit up to form small circles, they will look relaxed, quietly joyful, eyes and skin radiant. But right now, there's all the time in the world until lunch.

A LITTLE PHYSIOLOGY

Whether done in a group or one-to-one with a therapist, breathwork sessions can look dramatic. There can be crying, moaning, laughing, and sometimes shouting. Or they can appear so sedate, it seems like nothing is happening at all. But no matter what appears on the outside, there are few techniques as effective as breathwork for sloughing off the conditioning that keeps us trapped in our Small Self and taking us straight to the blissful state of oneness that is our Big Self.

Most of us take breathing for granted. We assume it will carry on in the background of our lives without much effort on our part. Until something goes wrong. Asthma, bronchitis, emphysema, or a plain old winter cold can quickly bring home to us just how vital breathing is to every aspect of life and how much it affects the quality of that life. After all, what else do we do 20,000 or so times a day?

In any twenty-four-hour period, the roughly 1,000 square feet of our lungs take in approximately 2,100 gallons of air, and the approximately four and a half gallons of blood that pass through our lungs carry oxygen to every cell in our body. Deprive the body of oxygen and it will die within minutes. What's less well known is the fact that approximately 70 percent of the body's waste is excreted through the lungs. Restrict the ability to exhale and toxins will build up in the body. [26, 27]

Breathing is controlled by the diaphragm, a powerful muscle that lies at the base of the lungs. When the diaphragm moves down into the abdomen, we inhale, and when it moves up into the chest, our lungs are forced to exhale. The base of the lungs is the area richest in blood supply; therefore, for physical health, it pays to breathe deeply into the abdomen. This is often called diaphragm or belly breathing, and it facilitates the most efficient exchange of blood gases—oxygen in, carbon dioxide out.

Middle-chest breathing, in comparison, is shallow and less efficient. Yet if you watch people breathe, this is where most of us focus our inhale. When people complete a breathwork session, their radiant, youthful skin and sparkly eyes are probably attributable to the increased oxygenation of the body that comes from the fuller, accelerated breathing.

Upper-chest or clavicular breathing is rarely done without conscious effort. Few people breathe right up into their collarbones unless they're practicing a breathing technique like the three-phase breath of yoga. Yet this is where we breathe when we're sobbing, frightened, or otherwise intensely emotionally activated.

The ability to clean the body and maximize its performance through breathing is well documented. Efficient breathing is essential to athletes, musicians, and performers. Diaphragm breathing is key to the management of the stress response, but there's an equally direct and dynamic link between breathing and psychology.

THE MIND-BODY CONTINUUM

The link between breathing and emotional states was first noticed by scientists in the 1930s, when researchers concluded that anxiety was a "respiratory neurosis" and stimulating the breathing could temporarily "restore sanity in schizophrenic patients."[28] The great, and at the time controversial, pioneer of breathwork, Wilhelm Reich, studied the way the human body responds to life events. If we tighten specific muscles in response to particular events, we set up a pattern of response that eventually shapes our posture. Reich called this "body armoring." The same thing happens with breathing. During periods of anxiety, for example, the inhale can become so shallow, it's almost imperceptible. Like body armoring, this alteration of the breathing pattern can be a way of holding the less pleasant aspects of life at bay, a kind of self-protection that wards off emotional pain. It too can become a fixed pattern. But while it may cushion the impact of life's punches, shallow or erratic breathing may also restrict our capacity for pleasure, even if it's just the pleasure of a full, free inhale.

The link between emotions and breathing has long been known to breathworkers. Recently this link has been substantiated by scientists in a joint study by the Université de Louvain and the Université du Québec à Montreal. As part of a controlled study, participants were asked to observe and report on their breathing patterns when feeling the emotions of anger, fear, sadness, and happiness. Sets of breathing instructions were drawn up based on these observations. These instructions were then given to a separate set of participants who were told to follow the breathing pattern and note their emotions. Sure enough, the breathing pattern for fear produced fear, anger breath produced anger, and so on.[29]

Breathing is governed by both the autonomic and the central nervous systems. This vital, automatic function can also be consciously controlled by us. This ability to breathe with awareness (also known as "conscious breathing"), this ability to change the way we breathe, makes breathing one of the most effective healing systems available.

Breathwork on the Inside

In the East, breathwork has been used for centuries to promote health, well-being, and spiritual growth. Because of this long history, the number of breathwork techniques is impossible to quantify. They range from slow, gentle breathing used in some forms of meditation to dramatic and vigorous breathing. The boundaries between techniques are fluid, but I think of breathwork under two headings: breathwork and accelerated breathwork.

By breathwork, I mean the vast range of controlled breathing exercises used in meditation, forms of yoga, and many stress management systems. These include alternate nostril breathing, three-phase breathing, and the counted breath exercises outlined in this chapter, to name but a few. Breathwork techniques can range from these simple exercises to what I call accelerated breathwork, which includes breathing techniques that change (usually increase but sometimes decrease) both the pace and/or volume of the inhale beyond the normal. Rebirthing, Holotropic, Transformational Breath, and some aspects of the Sudarshan Kriya Yoga (SKY) system fall into this category. Rebirthing, Holotropic, and Transformational Breath are

widely used around the world in both groups and one-to-one therapeutic sessions. Project Welcome Home Troops in the United States
uses SKY with veterans suffering from post-traumatic stress disorder
after returning from combat.[30] SKY combines breathwork with a
mantra and with movements of the stomach and abdominal muscles. The effects of this project have been researched by Dr. Emma
Seppala of Stanford University and Dr. Richard Davidson of the
University of Wisconsin–Madison.

People practice breathwork as a method of expanding their awareness and entering a state of oneness. They also practice breathwork as
a form of psychotherapy. As a psychotherapy, it's usually done with a
therapist. People come to breathwork with the same problems they
take to other forms of therapy—problems with relationships, low-
grade unhappiness, depression, all manner of issues. They also come
to breathwork out of a desire to explore and grow.

In breathwork, people find a multidimensional experience that
involves body, mind, and spirit. It offers an unparalleled opportunity
to shed the emotional and cognitive conditioning that blocks access
to the mystical. No clearly defined scientific reason exists to explain
why accelerated breathing leads to such powerful therapeutic and
mystical experiences. But a University of Toronto study of attention
and brain activity offers some insight.[31] The study distinguishes between externally and internally focused awareness. When we focus
our attention outside ourselves, as we do most of the time, the fron-
tal lobes of the neocortex are active. As we've seen, the neocortex is
the area of the brain that develops last and is associated with the
ability to conceptualize and judge. When we focus our attention inward, on our breathing, for example, older areas of the brain are activated, areas associated not with words, but with sensation, emotion, and physical experience. This study opens the possibility that
inward-focused attention, the kind of attention breathwork fosters,
can help us bypass our thinking mind so that we can access a deeper

level of awareness. It also gives us access to emotions and sense memories that lie beneath the surface of our outward-focused attention. This bypassing of the chattering, judging mind is exactly what happens in a breathwork session, and in a mystical state.

In breathwork sessions, we surrender to our Big Self, and in doing so, we let go of little, and often big, pieces of the baggage that has kept us tethered to our Small Self. The result is a deepening spiritual connection with life and a greater freedom in living that life. How does this work in practice? Let's follow a journey through a typical accelerated breathwork session.

For most people, a breathwork session follows a pattern or cycle of buildup, climax, and resolution or integration that mirrors the five practices. At the beginning of the session, the breather focuses on increasing their inhale, then exhaling fully. The natural pauses between breaths are eliminated, so inhale and exhale form a cycle, one flowing into the other. This accelerates the pace slightly. For some, this is easy. For others, it's physically uncomfortable. The role of the breathwork therapist is to provide instruction and encouragement if breathing becomes shallow or the breather decides to interrupt the process with conversation. Eventually, however, surrender comes. When this happens, the breath becomes full and rhythmic. The breather feels as if they are being breathed rather than breathing under their own steam. This frees the breather to focus inward so they can begin to work all five practices during the session.

Awareness in the Present Moment: Once the breathing pattern has been established, the breathwork experience becomes unique to the breather every time they engage in a breathwork session. The breather remains fully aware of their surroundings, but their inner awareness expands with every breath. They engage fully with the present moment and are, therefore, acutely aware of every sensation as it arises. Those sensations may be physical: localized discomfort, tingling, or waves of energy moving through the body, building up toward the head, and cascading back down. They may take the form of coldness or warmth, or a compulsion to move, to assume the fetal position, or to scratch or yawn.

Trust and Openness: Sensations may also be emotional—joy, sorrow, fear, shame, exuberance, anger, love, peace, anxiety—a full range of feelings. Emotions may be free-floating or come attached to a current life situation or to a memory—the memory of birth, for example. The breathwork technique called "Rebirthing" got its name and early theoretical framework from the surfacing of birth memories. If birth is remembered and the breather's mother is still alive and part of their life, the memory can be authenticated. Birth and womb time are generally the only forgotten memories to emerge in breathwork. Other memories that surface could easily be recalled at any time with a little skillful prompting. The difference between prompted recall in conversation and recall in breathwork is that the latter is a full-bodied experience—all the senses are engaged, not just the mind.

During an accelerated breathwork session, the breather often comes face to face with how they think and feel about themselves and life. These belief systems can govern our lives. In any circle of friends and acquaintances, for example, there are usually those for whom life seems effortless and others who struggle through an endless stream of complexities and difficulties. As soon as they fix one situation, something else goes wrong. If they dug deep enough, they would likely find some variation on the belief that "life is easy" or "life is a struggle." The belief system per se doesn't make life easy or difficult, but beliefs influence our behavior. Our behavior, in turn, shapes our experience. People who are regularly embroiled in struggle often make life more complex and difficult than it need be by their reactions and choices. They could make different, wiser choices, but because the belief that life is a struggle is active beneath the surface, they can't see any other way to behave.

This aspect of breathwork constitutes a master class in the third practice of Trust and Openness. The breather remains open to everything that surfaces in the session, trusting that all shall be well. This trust is important because when belief systems or thought patterns surface in breathwork, they too are full-body experiences and this holistic nature of breathwork is vitally important to its effectiveness. Everything is part of the breathwork process, and the breather trusts that process.

Growing from Adversity: *Gestalt* is a German word meaning "whole or complete form." In breathwork, we begin by bringing awareness to how we are in the present moment. How we are in the present is affected, in part, by unresolved events from our past. Those events have been left unresolved because we withdrew our awareness from them at the time they occurred. We often withdraw our awareness from the present moment. In extreme cases, this is called splitting off, and it's an essential trauma survival mechanism. Abused children survive by disassociating themselves from what's happening to them. Car crash victims often have no memory of the moment of impact. But we do a partial withdrawal of awareness on a regular basis. Partial withdrawal can take many forms. Sometimes it's through addictions—we eat for comfort rather than face the discomfort, for example. We can play out a role rather than risk vulnerability. We can withdraw into ideologies and belief systems. Or we can lose ourselves in anger, self-pity, gregariousness, or helplessness. We can hide behind almost anything. What we're doing is withdrawing awareness from the immediate situation, thus avoiding the discomfort, pain, or fear it arouses. In cases of extreme trauma, this may be our only option for survival, and revisiting the event needs to be done gradually and skillfully. But withdrawing awareness from what's happening is not the most effective long-term strategy for a full life.

Withdrawing awareness means we survive, but the issue remains unresolved. Our perception of the world is incomplete. Like a circle that hasn't been closed, past events strive for completion. Sigmund Freud called this the "repetition-compulsion syndrome"—we're doomed to repeat what we have not resolved. We experience this syndrome as everything turning out the same old way despite our best effort to change old patterns.

During breathwork, awareness is restored. The breather experiences the session fully, 100 percent engagement. The key is to be fully present to the experience. No matter how painful the emotion, no matter how uncomfortable the physical sensation, the breather stays with it. She works the third practice of Trust and Openness. A skilled breathwork therapist knows how to support the breather in maintaining their focus.

The climax of the breathwork cycle is when emotions are at their height, sensations are strong, and belief systems are starkly present. Session climax can be a difficult few minutes, a kind of mini dark night of the soul. But it is literally a few minutes, all made possible by awareness and embracing what is—here, now, in the eternal present. This ability to surrender to inner reality rests on trust—trust in the breath, the process, knowing that embracing this darkness without judgment makes the spiritual and psychological magic of resolution happen. The circle is closed, the form made whole.

Oneness: The final phase of a breathwork session is a period of delicious calm. Catharsis has happened followed by resolution, and this final stage brings integration. Changes have taken place within the breather. Old emotions and memories have emerged, and because the breather has seen them through with awareness instead of distancing herself from them, they have been resolved. Previously obscured belief systems have come to the fore and, in the process, have lost some of their grip. The breather herself has grown and changed over the course of the session.

During the final phase, these changes permeate the entire body. Breathing returns to normal, and the body is calm, deeply relaxed, often tingling with waves of energy. At this point, the breather often moves to another level of spiritual experience: the state of oneness. This phase should not be interrupted. It's not just intensely blissful, it's where change is consolidated and made real in the body. The breather herself will know when to open her eyes and rejoin the world.

Accelerated breathwork is the five practices in action at once. It offers a gateway into oneness and is an invaluable tool as we proceed through the rest of this book. In chapters 8 through 14, we will explore in detail the issues that hold us back from living fully. We will learn how to put our spiritual experience into action in daily life. But if we want to put the wisdom of the contemplative mind into action, it's helpful, and often essential, to have the support of a spiritual technique or therapy. If you think breathwork may be your technique of choice, here is some more detail on the forms of breathwork that are available.

FORMS OF BREATHWORK

Accelerated breathwork can be done in one-to-one sessions or groups. Accelerated breathwork techniques are usually learned through working with a breathwork therapist. One-to-one breathwork sessions also vary widely in structure. Some therapists operate with minimal talk, and the entire focus of the session is the breathwork. Others have a period of talking with the client prior to and after the breathing session. Some therapists use focused bodywork, movement, artwork, or music before the session to prepare the breather for their breathwork experience, during the session to enhance the process, or as a method of grounding the breathwork experience after the breathing portion of the session has been completed. There is no single perfect breathing technique. As with forms of meditation, the breather uses whatever pattern of breathing works for them. Breathwork can generally be done alone once the client has mastered the technique, but the experience differs from breathwork done in the presence of a therapist.

Rebirthing: Rebirthing Breathwork was developed by Leonard Orr in the 1970s. The name "Rebirthing" comes from the fact that Orr experienced his birth during a self-guided rebirthing session. As a result, during early years of the therapy, rebirthers focused on the psychological effects of birth as the theoretical framework for rebirthing. This has since broadened to include all life experiences. The breathwork session at the Global Inspiration Conference described near the beginning of this chapter was a rebirthing session.

Rebirthing uses a full breathing pattern in which air fills the lungs from abdomen to collarbones. Breathing is connected so there are no pauses. The emphasis is on the inhale, and the exhale is uncontrolled, much like a sigh. Rebirthing can be carried out in one-to-one sessions or in groups. It can be done alone after learning the technique from a therapist.

Holotropic Breathwork: Holotropic Breathwork was developed by Stanislav and Christina Grof. It uses an intensified breathing technique, which can become quite vigorous. One-to-one sessions are available, but Holotropic Breathwork is most commonly done in groups. In groups, participants pair up. One of the pair breathes and the other observes and supports the breather. Then the roles are reversed.

The therapists who lead the group often use bodywork as part of the session. This means they apply pressure to parts of the breather's body while he is breathing. Loud, carefully chosen music is also used. At the end of a Holotropic Breathwork sessions, breathers use artwork, the drawing of a personal mandala, to ground the experience.

Radiance Breathwork: Radiance Breathwork was developed by Gay Hendricks. The technique is generally done in one-to-one sessions with a trained facilitator/therapist. The therapist helps the client find the pattern and pace of breathing that will promote relaxation and surrender to the breathing process. Before breathwork commences, the client sets an intention for the session. The therapist may also use bodywork during the breathing session.

Transformational Breath: This form of breathwork was developed by Judith Kravitz. Breathing is full and relaxed and begins in the lower abdomen. Breathing is circular in that the pauses between inhale and exhale are eliminated. Other techniques, such as focused touch and sound and the use of personal intention, are incorporated into the breathwork. Transformational Breath can take place in group or one-to-one sessions and can be done alone after learning the technique from a therapist.

SOME BREATHING EXERCISES

The following breathwork exercises will be referenced throughout the rest of this book as experiential techniques to help you put the five practices to work in your life.

EXERCISE 12: TWENTY CONNECTED BREATHS

This is a classic introduction to accelerated breathing such as Rebirthing. Sit comfortably with your spine erect and supported. Do a quick scan of your body, noticing areas of tension, skin sensations, and energy levels as well as your mood. Breathing either through your nose or mouth, inhale as fully as you can. Make sure your breath fills your lungs from belly to collarbones. When you have inhaled to capacity, exhale immediately in an uncontrolled manner, as if you were sighing. Just let the weight of your chest and gravity empty your lungs. As soon as you have exhaled, inhale again. This eliminates the pauses in your breathing cycle and will naturally quicken the pace. Repeat the inhale and exhale twenty times. You may begin to feel lightheaded. This is a normal effect of this kind of breathing and will pass after you complete your twenty breaths. When you finish the exercise, take note of how your body feels. Do you detect any changes in temperature, aliveness, skin sensation, etc.? Breathing through your mouth during this exercise tends to facilitate emotional awareness, while breathing through the nose tends to facilitate clarity of thought. This is a tendency, not a hard and fast rule.

EXERCISE 13: ALTERNATE NOSTRIL BREATHING

This is a well-known, ancient breathing technique for relaxation and calming the mind. Again, seat yourself comfortably with your spine erect and supported. With your right hand in front of your face, place your forefinger and middle finger on your forehead between your eyebrows. Close your left nostril with the pressure of your ring finger and breathe slowly through your right nostril. Then use your thumb to close your right nostril. Remove your ring finger from your left nostril and exhale. As soon as you have exhaled, inhale again slowly through your left nostril. Then close your left nostril and exhale and inhale through the right nostril. It sounds complicated, but once you follow the instructions for a few breaths, it will come naturally to you. Keep breathing this way for at least five minutes and then for as long as you want. You may find one nostril more open than the other. This too is normal and will change throughout the day. When you have finished your breathing exercise, notice how your body feels and if your mind has come to rest.

EXERCISE 14: COUNTED BREATH

This exercise is often used for managing stage fright. Position yourself comfortably, standing, sitting, or lying down.

• Inhale through your nose for a count of four.

• Hold your breath for a count of four.

• Exhale for a count of four.

• Hold your breath for a count of four.

• Repeat the cycle until you feel calm.

EXERCISE 15: THREE-PHASE BREATHING

Sit or lie down comfortably. Place one hand on your abdomen and one hand on your chest. Breathe slowly through your nose. Bring air deep into your abdomen until you feel your belly rise under your hand. Allow the air to fill your mid-chest, the area around your heart, and then your upper chest, the area beneath your collarbones. When the entire expanse of your lungs has been filled with air, begin to exhale slowly in reverse order. Empty your upper chest first, then the heart area, and then your belly. Once you master this technique, it works smoothly and naturally and is an excellent treatment for stress and anxiety.

Psychotherapy/Therapy

The term "psychotherapy" (which is used interchangeably with "therapy") refers to a vast range of techniques that are used to promote psychological health and personal growth. Some forms of psychotherapy use breathwork, and in my opinion, breathwork is a form of psychotherapy. Other psychotherapies employ art, movement, play, and visualization, as well as skillful questioning and feedback techniques.

Traditionally, psychotherapy focused on psychological development and did not necessarily incorporate an awareness of the spiritual dimension. More recently developed psychotherapeutic approaches merge the psychological with the spiritual. I do not distinguish between psychological and spiritual growth. When we resolve Small Self psychological issues, we open to the spiritual, to our Big Self. In the process of opening up to the spiritual, we frequently resolve psychological problems. However, more mainstream schools of psychotherapy may draw a clearer distinction between the psychological and the spiritual.

Psychotherapy is most frequently carried out in one-to-one sessions, but group psychotherapy, couples, and family/systemic therapy are also available. A traditional psychotherapy session is slightly less than an hour, but some forms of therapy—therapies that incorporate breathwork, for example—take longer.

No one form of therapy is "faster" or "deeper" than another. When choosing a form of therapy, we need to decide whether we respond best to sitting in a chair and talking with our therapist, or whether we find techniques that involve movement, breathing, or imagination more suitable.

FORMS OF PSYCHOTHERAPY

Psychoanalysis: The theory and techniques of psychoanalytic therapy were pioneered by Sigmund Freud, the grandfather of psychotherapy. This therapy is based on Freud's map of the mind, which includes the dimension of the unconscious.

Psychoanalysis explores the unconscious forces at play in our lives. The methods used include free association of words, dream interpretation, and the analysis of resistance and transference. Transference is the process of relating to someone in the present as if they were a significant person from our past. Transference between client and analyst is explored as part of therapy. Psychoanalysis is usually regarded as a longer-term therapy.

Humanistic Psychotherapy: Humanistic psychology and therapy was developed by Carl Rogers, Abraham Maslow, and others in reaction to psychoanalysis. Humanistic therapy takes the approach that the client plays a role in creating her own problems, and by taking responsibility for that role, she is empowered to solve those problems.

This approach is based on the belief that human beings are basically good. If we are allowed to grow uninterrupted by traumatic life events, we will naturally gravitate toward wholeness and goodness. Problems are created when that natural development is blocked or driven off course by life events. Humanistic therapy is focused on supporting the client to become aware of the role she plays in perpetuating her problems and to learn that she has the power to resolve those problems.

A wide range of therapies fall under the category of humanistic. In addition, many humanistic therapists mix and match techniques from various schools of therapy. The best-known approaches in this category are Carl Rogers's person-centered therapy and Fritz Perls's Gestalt therapy.

- **Person-Centered Therapy:** Person-centered therapy emphasizes the relationship between client and therapist. Essential elements of this relationship are genuineness, authenticity, unconditional (nonjudgmental) acceptance by the therapist, and an openness to vulnerability and empathy. The therapist's role is to support the development of a relationship within which the client can feel safe to explore themselves and to grow. Techniques include questioning, reflecting back to the client what they have said, summarizing the content of the session for the client, and focusing on the client's strengths.

- **Gestalt Therapy:** Gestalt therapy focuses on developing awareness of feelings and behaviors as they occur in the present rather than the past. The goal of therapy is to expand self-awareness. With awareness, the client can begin to meet his own needs. While problems may have originated in the client's past, the therapy focuses on how those problems manifest in the here and now. Techniques include role-play, body awareness, beating pillows, and the "empty chair." When practicing the empty chair technique, the client imagines a significant person associated with a problem in their life, or the problem itself, to be sitting in a chair in the therapy room. The client then talks to the person in the chair as if they were really present in the room.

Cognitive Behavioral Therapy (CBT): Cognitive behavioral therapy is based on the belief that a change in the way we think will lead to a change in the way we feel and behave. A significant aspect of the therapy, therefore, involves the development of awareness around thought processes and how to change them. Techniques include relaxation training, reframing problems from a different perspective, thought management, and homework assignments. For clients with significant fears, CBT can also include controlled exposure to the source of those fears. A client with an inordinate fear of meeting new people, for example, may be given a homework assignment to say hello to a stranger. CBT therapists are more directive in their approach than humanistic therapists, and clients are active participants in their own therapy. CBT is noted for its success with depression, phobias, and anxiety disorders. More recently it has joined forces with mindfulness meditation.

Systemic Therapy: This approach focuses on the individual as part of a system of relationships. Other forms of psychotherapy focus on the individual client's thought processes, history, experience, and so forth. Systemic therapy approaches individual problems from the perspective of the network of relationships in the client's life. Patterns of relating may help maintain the problems the client has come to therapy to resolve. So while systemic therapists work with individuals as well as with families and groups, they approach the client's issues from a systemic perspective.

Note: What I've just described are four broad categories of therapy, four therapeutic approaches. Within each category we find so many variations and combinations of techniques that the boundaries between therapies can become confusingly blurred. It's important not to get stuck trying to understand the intricacies of the different therapeutic approaches. Time will be much better spent finding a therapist with whom the client feels secure yet challenged, then get on with the work of therapy.

Choosing a Therapist/Breathworker

I have addressed breathwork, psychotherapy, and spiritual techniques separately, but in reality, all three categories can flow into each other, particularly breathwork and therapy.

With both breathwork and therapy, the choice of a therapist is at least as important as the choice of therapy, so please read this information about choosing a therapist before you research therapists or breathworkers in your area.

A wealth of research exists to show that the relationship between the therapist and client is one of the most important therapeutic factors in psychotherapy. The quality of the therapist-client relationship outweighs both the techniques used and the theoretical approach of the therapist. There is no similar research for breathwork, but if there were, I suspect it would weight the client–breathwork therapist relationship highly. Choosing a therapist, therefore, is at least as important as choosing a technique. The first session with a therapist offers the opportunity to explore the fit between therapist and client.

During the first session, the therapist and client begin the process of developing a rapport, the foundation on which the therapeutic relationship will be built. Trust and rapport require more than one session to develop, but a lot can be learned in the first meeting. The client and therapist can discuss techniques and approaches in detail and, at the same time, get to know each other.

In my experience, clients don't ask too many questions about credentials, but a good therapist will be open to talking about their training and experiences. Most therapists are affiliated with a licensing or registration body that can be checked online by the client. Registration body websites are a good place to find a therapist. In some countries, breathwork therapists are similarly registered, but this is not always the case. The most reliable way to find a therapist is through referral from someone who knows, trusts, and may have already worked with that therapist.

SPIRITUAL TECHNIQUES

The array of practices and techniques that promote spiritual awareness and mystical experience is truly vast. The field includes all forms of meditation, yoga, dance, movement, art, prayer, and more. Some of these techniques may be led by a teacher (yoga, for example) or a group meditation leader. But the therapeutic relationship—the relationship that develops between a client and therapist during breathwork or psychotherapy—is not present. In fact, a spiritual technique is often a solitary activity.

As with therapies and breathwork techniques, the key is to find the one that suits your temperament and way of working. If you are able to sit for long periods of time and focus your mind on one thing, a mantra- or object-focused meditation may be suitable. If you need more activity, then breath-based meditation or walking meditation may be a better choice. Or you may prefer a physically demanding practice such as yoga or dance.

Mantra Meditation: A mantra is a word or image that becomes the focus of awareness during meditation. The word used usually holds no meaning for the meditator—the word "Om," for example. The mantra can be said silently or chanted aloud. Transcendental

Meditation (TM) is probably the most famous form of mantra meditation in the West. When practicing TM, the meditator assumes a comfortable seated position and repeats their mantra silently for approximately twenty minutes at a time. When attention drifts, the meditator refocuses on the mantra. Centering Prayer, developed by Father Thomas Keating, is a Christian version of mantra mediation. In Centering Prayer, the meditator focuses on a word or phrase that represents their willingness to surrender to the presence of God.

Mindfulness Meditation: Jon Kabat-Zinn defines mindfulness meditation as "paying attention on purpose, in the present moment, and non-judgmentally to whatever is arising inwardly and outwardly."[32] Mindfulness is about being fully present to the now and to whatever is happening in the now. If we are walking, we pay full attention to the sensations of walking. If we are typing, we pay full attention to the feel of our fingers on the keyboard. Whatever we're doing, we're fully present to it. When we sit down to a meditation session, we pay attention to the sensations, thoughts, and feelings we experience in the present moment. We can use our breathing as the focus of attention, feeling every sensation of inhale and exhale. When thoughts about the past or future arise, we attend to how they appear in the present. We don't judge anything that comes into our awareness.

Movement Meditation: For people who respond best to more active meditation, several forms of movement can be used to focus awareness in the present moment. I find slow, mindful walking to be the most effective for me. Dance can also be used as a meditation practice. Well-known forms of dance meditation include ecstatic dance and the five rhythms, developed by Gabrielle Roth. When using movement as a form of meditation, it's important to fully inhabit our bodies, to experience every physical sensation, every footfall, every turn and bend, until, through movement, our mind stills and we experience pure existence in the present moment.

Object-Focused Meditation: Some people meditate best when they focus on an object, such as a candle, fire, flower, or sculpture. Any object will do as long as it doesn't provoke us into thinking. The object works in the same way as a mantra. It fills our mind, and when we catch ourselves thinking, we bring our attention back to the object. I find object-focused meditation particularly effective when I combine staring at a candle with mindfulness of my own breathing. Music can also be an object on which to meditate. When we are fully present to music, we can feel the sounds physically.

Visualization: In visualization, we use our visual imagination to take us to a desired place. This could be a physical location where we feel safe and at peace, or it could be an event or outcome we desire in our lives. For many people, visualizing themselves actually working in the job they are seeking or being in the relationship they would like to experience is helpful in propelling them toward that outcome. I have used visualization mostly for stress management or to generate feelings of safety, peace, and love that my clients or members of my personal development classes felt they lacked in their lives. In either case, visualizations work best when we employ all of our senses—we don't just look around the world we've created in our imagination; we also hear, smell, taste, and touch that world. In practicing visualization, it can be helpful to buy one of the many professionally recorded visualizations available in bookstores and online, but you can also record your own voice. Or you can visualize in silence.

EXERCISE 16: VISUALIZATION

For this exercise, you will need a comfortable place to be alone, a place where you won't be interrupted. Relax into a comfortable chair or lie on a bed or mat. Close your eyes and take some deep breaths into your belly to clear your mind.

Picture yourself descending a luxuriously carpeted stair-case. Move slowly. Feel your bare feet sinking into the carpet, your hand sliding along the stair rail. At the bottom of the stairs, you find yourself in a hallway. Take the time to look around at the colors of the hallway, the textures, the sensation of the floor beneath your feet. Across the hallway you see a wooden door. Notice the rich, warm glow of the wood. Move toward the door and touch the handle. Feel its smoothness, its temperature, the pressure on your hand as you open the door and step across the threshold.

On the other side of the door, you find a beach (or any place of your choosing—a garden, woodland, meadow, mountains, underwater grotto, etc.). You are alone on this beach, and any chores or responsibilities you have in life are being taken care of by people you trust. Look around you and slowly drink in the colors and shapes. See the sweep of golden sand skirted by waves. Perhaps there are sand dunes, coastal grasses and flow-ers, or purple mountains in the distance. Feel the sand beneath your feet, the fresh sea air on your skin, the warmth of sun-shine, and the touch of a gentle breeze. Hear the sound of waves rolling to shore. Perhaps you hear birds calling to each other or the breeze rustling the grasses. Can you taste the saltiness in the air and smell the freshness of the breeze and the fragrance of the ocean?

Decide what you want to do on this beach. Lie down in the sand and feel the warmth of the sun on your skin, the sand sift-ing through your fingers. Paddle in the waves, and feel the cool water lapping at your ankles. You're free to stay on this beach as long as you like. You're free to paddle or swim, to sunbathe or explore tide pools, to sleep or read. The day is yours to do with as you please. Enjoy it. And when you feel it's time to leave, take one last look around the beach, breathe deeply of the sea air, and slowly open your eyes. Take as long as you need to ease your way out of the visualized world and back into your surroundings.

Yoga: Yoga is an ancient Hindu philosophy that facilitates mystical union or oneness through complete awareness and mastery of the mind. In the West, yoga has become synonymous with a series of exercises or postures that have often, to varying degrees, become detached from their philosophical and spiritual roots. When practicing the postures of yoga, our mind can become so fully engaged in the present-moment experience that we enter a state of stillness and peace. However, if we approach yoga as a form of exercise, a workout, we can lose out on the meditative effects of the practice. Yoga is widely popular, and classes are easy to locate. A good yoga center will provide explanations of the various forms of yoga available.

The Laundry: Jack Kornfield wrote a very useful book called *After the Ecstasy, the Laundry.* The title is a good reminder that even the most mundane tasks can be used as a meditation if they are done mindfully. Washing dishes, doing the ironing, mowing the lawn, or raking leaves in the garden can all be used to quiet our mind and open the door to stillness. The key is to do whatever we're doing fully and completely, with 100 percent attention.

7

THE CIRCLE OF EFFECT:
How We Shape Our Own Lives

Nothing happens until something moves.
~ALBERT EINSTEIN

When a potter shapes a lump of damp clay into a vase or a bowl, he does so by performing a series of actions: throwing the clay on the wheel, pressing a foot on the pedal that controls the spinning, and molding the clay with deft movements of hands and fingers. For a bowl, the hands move one way, and for a vase, another. Or the potter may refrain from moving a finger, and that too has an effect.

We shape our lives in the same manner. We cannot directly change another person, but we can choose how we act and react to them. This, in turn, affects how they behave toward us. This confluence of action and reaction shapes the contours of our lives and makes us, at a minimum, the co-architects of our destiny. Understanding and embracing this fact is fundamental to putting the five practices into action in life. Otherwise we will be working against ourselves.

This dynamic of co-creation is easier to see in others than in ourselves, and easier still to spot in children and animals. For fourteen years, I had the pleasure of living with a scruffy little white-and-black dog nobody would ever describe as good-looking. Her name was Woodie, and she never let her lack of beauty get in the way of a good time. Whenever someone came to the house, with no hesitation Woodie would walk up to them, sit at their feet, and stare serenely into their eyes. It never failed. Within minutes, the visitor would reach down to pet the dog and talk to her as if she were a baby. The dog I have now, Tooshar, is sleek and glossy and, in doggie terms, a looker. But Tooshar does not assume a God-given right to affection. She's tentative and unsure and approaches people cautiously, even skittishly. Unlike with Woodie, people instinctively reach out to touch Tooshar's glossy coat, but her cautious, jerky movements make them recoil just as quickly. Tooshar is a loving dog, but she gets far less affection than the much less beautiful Woodie—and it's all her own doing.

Children are just as transparent. It is easy to see the cautious, shy child skirt the edges of a group while her more confident friends grab attention. Even at such a young age, a child's actions shape her social world. Troubled children can appear relentless in their drive to alienate adult caregivers who are trying hard to love them.

Each one of us exercises a similar influence on our own life every day. For people who feel helplessly trapped in circumstances that seem beyond their control, this power to influence can be difficult to recognize, let alone acknowledge. But the most reliable and sustainable way to effect change is to recognize our part in shaping the life we have right now. This recognition is the first step to expanding into a richer, fuller way of being. The tools we use to shape our lives are simple and straightforward:

- We act or refrain from acting.
- We speak or refrain from speaking.
- We speak silently and powerfully with our bodies.
- We carry with us an energy that communicates with others without any of us realizing communication is happening.

ACTIONS

I once worked with a woman named Diana who complained that the adult son with whom she lived expected her to take care of him as if he were still a child. He demanded dinner served on his schedule, his laundry done and folded, his room cleaned. Diana struggled to understand why this child whom she loved so much would treat her so badly. We worked through months of intensive self-esteem building, but the relationship with her son remained unchanged. In his book *Your Erroneous Zones*, Wayne Dyer talks about the ways we teach other people how to treat us. No matter what angle we approached the situation from, Diana couldn't identify the ways in which she had taught her son that treating his mother with disrespect was acceptable.

One September afternoon, Diana arrived for our session bubbly and smiling. The previous evening, she had been weeding in the garden, a job her son refused to tackle. Diana heard him shouting to her from the deck at the rear of their house. He was going out for the evening and demanded she cook his dinner before he left. Diana was about to put down her hand spade and rush into the kitchen to start cooking, but something inside her snapped—at least that's how she described it. She told him to get his own dinner or eat out, and continued weeding. Her son stared at her for several minutes, but Diana kept on working. Then, without speaking, he left the house. They never spoke about the incident again, but it was the beginning of a radical change in their relationship. The simple act of meeting his demands gave her son permission to make those demands. Once Diana recognized how her own actions and inaction shaped the relationship, change came rapidly.

Our actions may seem insignificant at the time, so insignificant that we don't even notice or question what we're doing. Later, however, we notice the consequence of those actions and puzzle over how things got to be this way. When, for example, we habitually tell our children they will have to go to their room if they don't stop squabbling and then don't act upon our threat, we store up trouble for ourselves in the future. Years later, when those children have grown into teenagers who stay out late, we wonder why they've suddenly become so difficult. But they haven't changed. They have simply learned what we taught them: that there are no consequences. We are the ones left facing the consequence of our own inaction.

EXERCISE 17: ACTIONS AND CONSEQUENCES

a) You will need a pen and paper for this exercise. Pick a situation in your life when you had the choice to take action but *you held back*. What were the consequences? (They could be positive or negative.) Here's an example:

> **Situation:** *Margaret was introduced to a woman at a dinner party. The woman had an opening at her company. Margaret was looking for a job in the same field, so the woman asked her to send her résumé immediately because interviews were already underway. The next day, Margaret was invited to go skiing with friends, so she didn't send in her résumé until it was too late.*

> **Consequences:** *Margaret was unemployed for another three months. She got a job at a lower wage and had to take in a roommate because she couldn't pay the rent on her own. The roommate introduced her to the man who would become her husband. It could have been completely different had she sent in her résumé.*

b) Pick a situation in your life where you had the choice to take action or not and *you took action*. What were the consequences? How has that decision played out in your life?

WORDS

Our words also shape our world. When we say no to something we don't want to do, we set a clear boundary. This boundary shapes our relationship with the person we said no to. When we say yes even though we mean no, that too shapes the future of our relationship, but in a different way. Equally influential is what we do not say. When we refrain from speaking to someone at a party, we forgo the possibilities inherent in developing a connection with that person. When we hold back from presenting ourselves to others, we become, in a way, invisible. The inevitable consequence of holding back is that someone else gets noticed, makes connections, and reaps the rewards, and we do not. It's tempting and very common to complain about how other people always get the goodies, never us. But with that little hesitation, that holding back of speech and eye contact, we set the process of being ignored in motion.

EXERCISE 18: WORDS AND CONSEQUENCES

c) Have you ever kept silent when you could have spoken up? What were the consequences for you or others? How did keeping silent that time play out in your life? (Could be positive or negative.)

d) Have you ever spoken up and regretted doing so? What were the consequences of your speaking? Trace the effect of what you said as it played out in your life. (Could be positive or negative.)

Body Language

Estimates vary of how much of our communication is nonverbal, but for the communication of emotions it generally hovers around 80 percent. This means that no matter how much we craft what we say, around four-fifths of our communication has nothing to do with the meaning of the words we speak. The message comes through our body, our facial expressions, the way we hold our shoulders, the straightness of our spine, what we do with our arms and legs, and, most of all, our eye contact. Body language is culturally influenced. What is polite in one culture (eye contact, for example) is disrespectful in another. But cultural differences aside, our bodies tell others whether we are open or closed to them, aggressive or passive, confident or fearful.

At social events, our body language tells people to come close or stay away. Taking up a position where we can't be seen or looking away at a critical moment are both unspoken "keep out" signs. Placing ourselves in the flow of traffic, smiling, facing squarely into a group, and standing with open arms all invite people to say hello.

One of the best ways to understand the effect of body language is to observe our own responses to other people. How do we react to someone who won't look at us, who slouches into a room and shrugs when we ask them a question? How do we react to an open posture, a smile, eye contact? If we've ever interviewed someone for a job, we know how rapidly we react to the way the interviewee moves across the room, the way he sits, and his level of eye contact. Chances are the interviewee's body language will influence our decision.

Body language is one of the most powerful tools we use to co-create our lives. The messages we give through our bodies influence our daily experiences, and those small day-to-day experiences add up to a life. Whether we are satisfied or dissatisfied with our life, our body language, words, and actions have played a major role in making it what it is right now.

EXERCISE 19: PEOPLE-WATCHING

Find a spot where you can people-watch discreetly. Choose individual passersby at random. Watch how they hold themselves, their stature, how they hold their heads and move their arms, the expressions on their faces. Do you feel drawn to them or not? What in their body language attracts you, what turns you off, and what leaves you unaffected?

EXERCISE 20: WHAT AM I THINKING?

This is a fun exercise to do with friends. I've used it with most of my personal development groups and it never fails to surprise people. Gather one or more friends together. Tell them this will be a silent exercise and you want them to watch your body and face. Explain that you will be thinking a particular thought (don't tell them what it is) and that you will at some point switch to another thought. Ask them to raise their hand at the point when you switch to the second thought.

Stand before your friend(s) and repeat silently: "My life is dull and boring." Keep repeating this sentence to yourself for at least one minute. Then switch to "I love my life," and repeat it with every inhale, breathing it deep into your stomach. If you are fully engaged with the sentences you are repeating to yourself, your friends will notice when you switch over to the second sentence. They will likely notice it a short while after you make the switch because the change takes time to show itself in your body. Ask them to explain what they saw that indicated you had "changed your mind."

ENERGY

For the most part, our bodies speak without our permission. When we do try to control our physical communication, we can appear stiff and inauthentic. While it can be difficult to rein in our body language, for most people it's next to impossible to control the energetic communication that emanates from what, in Eastern thinking, is called our aura.

In Western systems of anatomy, the outer boundary of our body is its coating of skin. In Eastern systems, we are not so clearly delineated. Beyond the visible physical body is the aura or energy field. The aura can be photographed by a method called Kirlian photography, and some people can see the swirl of colors that surrounds each person. I have glimpsed auras from time to time, but for most Westerners, the aura is invisible. But just because we can't see it doesn't mean we're not attuned to it. If you've ever become aware of someone behind you even though you neither saw nor heard them enter the room, you have felt another person's energy field, or aura.

Many years ago, I stocked shelves part-time in supermarkets. Every so often, an executive from the head office would swoop into the store. Their presence was felt immediately. That presence wasn't just due to the expensive suits the executives wore. Without doing or saying anything, those executives exuded authority, confidence, even brashness. They carried their authority and power in their aura, and that power evoked an alarming degree of subservience in the people around them.

EXERCISE 21: PERSONAL SPACE

This is another fun exercise to do with friends. You can work with one other person, but the ideal is a group of four or more. Stand at opposite sides of the room. One person remains in place while the other walks slowly toward her. The person who is standing still raises her hand when the walker gets too close. The space left between the two people when the walker stops moving is the personal space of the one standing still. Then reverse the roles. After each person has had a turn walking and standing still, walk around each other and play with the space between you, test it. What's it like for someone to come too close? What's it like to be told to stay farther away than you would like? Most of all, how do you know when the other person is crossing into your personal space? What are the sensations you pick up on that tell you the other person is too close?

CIRCLE OF EFFECT

Words, deeds, body language, and the nature of our aura or energy field are the tools we use to shape our existence. If we wish to make changes in our lives, we need to change the way we use our tools. Change is inherent in growth; we cannot grow without something changing. The catch is that *we* are the ones who have to do the changing, not other people. And this is the source of our personal power. We don't have to hang around waiting for other people to change. We can make change happen, and we do that by embodying the five practices and putting them to work in our lives.

So let's begin with an emotion that has touched most of our lives, sometimes subtly, sometimes dramatically: fear.

8

BREAKING FREE
FROM FEAR

*It may be hard for an egg to turn into a bird: it would be a jolly sight
harder for it to learn to fly while remaining an egg… you cannot go on
indefinitely being just an ordinary, decent egg.
We must be hatched or go bad.*

~C. S. LEWIS, *MERE CHRISTIANITY*

Early in my therapy practice, I learned to recognize when someone
wants relief from pain but will shy away from making the changes
that would take the pain away. This reluctance shows in "Yes, but…"
responses, in talking slightly off the point, in suddenly jumping to a
new topic. I often marvel at clients who come to therapy knowing
what they want, and within a few sessions experience deep and lasting transformation. I have done the same myself: grasped the opportunity for change with both hands and made the most of it. On other

occasions—far rarer, I'm happy to say—I have had that "Yes, but ... Let's talk about something else" reaction. I've analyzed both responses from many angles, searching for that quiet, small difference that has such huge ramifications in a person's life. The only answer I can come up with is fear.

Nearly two millennia ago, the Bible advised us repeatedly to "be not afraid." Perhaps the reason that instruction appears so frequently is that fear is probably our biggest barrier to experiencing oneness. For many people, fear is a constant companion, and for others, an occasional visitor. Either way, fear and its low-lying cousin anxiety can hold us back from full engagement with life, can cause us to pass on golden opportunities, and can sour our enjoyment of even the smallest pleasures.

If we want to manage fear in our lives, many of the changes we need to make are internal. And here is where we encounter the double bind of fear. Not only does fear hold us back from life, it also holds us back from making the inner change that would free us from its grip, from lighting the candle that would take away our darkness. So let's begin our exploration of fear with the fear of change.

Fear of Change

The step that sets change in motion, that lights the candle, is a step into the unknown. If life has taught us that the unknown is a high-risk gamble, then it's logical to stay where we are. Darkness is familiar. It may be far from satisfying or safe, but it's what we know. When we weigh what we know against taking a step into the risky unknown, we often opt to remain "unhatched."

Sometimes it's possible to find the origins of this fear. It can go back to childhood, or to the biggest change of all—birth. A traumatic birth can undermine our ability to face change for years to come. Fear of change can also be located in our present circumstances and in the effect change could have on the people in our lives.

Often the issues that limit our ability to flow with life are so shrouded in fear that we have great difficulty going anywhere near them. What makes it even trickier is that we also insulate ourselves from the fear itself. The insulation is so effective, we may not even feel afraid. We catch sight of the fear only in dreams or in fleeting moments when an image passes through our awareness and is gone.

Whatever the reason behind the inertia, the first step must be taken. We can read books, take a pill, practice meditation, or commit to an endless range of therapies, but none of it will make much difference until we find within us that small nugget of courage that allows us to take the first step. The first step can be a tiny, almost imperceptible outward change in something we do or don't do. More often it's an inner shift that nobody else can see. It's a change of mind, a change of attitude, an opening to the possibility that the way we see things may not be the only way to look at life. Sometimes change begins with a recognition that we don't know nearly as much as we think we do.

Every step on the spiritual journey can bring a level of anxiety that, if we don't recognize it for what it is, can prevent us from going any further. This is normal. We know instinctively that once we take a step, the rest of the edifice we have built up around us must shift to accommodate even a small change. "Whenever we're led out of normalcy into sacred space, it's going to feel like suffering," author Richard Rohr says. But "if that readiness isn't there, we won't enter into sacred space."[33] Courage is the willingness to take that step, even though we are afraid and even though we do not know where it will lead.

The Third Practice: Trust: For those who find trust difficult, dealing with the fear of change can seem insurmountable, like boxing a shadow we can hardly see. However, if we have a willingness to explore, we can chip away at fear ever so gradually, making changes in manageable doses. Transformation often happens quietly, one little step of trust at a time. It can seem frustratingly slow. But if we look behind us, we see that all those little steps have accumulated into a journey. Then one day, when we take another backward glance, we wonder at the person we once were, the person we now are, and what on earth we were so afraid of. But to get to this point, it's helpful to break down our fear of change into manageable pieces so we can begin to chip away at that wall. Here is an exercise that can help you take that first step.

EXERCISE 22: UNDERSTANDING FEAR OF CHANGE

Find a time and place where you can be alone and won't feel rushed or be interrupted. You'll need a pen, paper, and a comfortable place to sit. When you're ready, begin a review of your current life situation. Are there changes you'd like to make that you're not making? You think about the change, you want it, but you're just not making it happen. (You may or may not be aware of the emotion of fear in relation to this particular change.) Choose one change you desire but that's not happening for you right now. Begin with something manageable. Leave the big life transformations, if you have any, for later. Describe your desired change.

Here's an example:

> **My Desired Change:** *I've taken on a lot of new responsibilities at work, and I want a pay raise to reflect this. I know I should ask for a raise, but I keep putting it off.*

Now put your pen down and practice the twenty connected breaths (exercise 12) from chapter 6, breathing through your nose. Don't be too concerned about counting the breaths. Instead, bring your awareness to the area of your belly and heart. You're not looking for any particular sensation. You're simply practicing awareness, letting your Inner Witness come forward. When you feel anchored in your body and your Inner Witness is ready to take the lead, pick up your pen and keep answering the question "When I think about (the change you want to make), I'm afraid of ..." Here's an example:

> **When I think about asking for a raise, I feel ...**
> *Angry, bored, shaky, giddy, embarrassed, ashamed, too big for my boots, afraid they'll say no, afraid of what they'll think of me, I could end up fired, with no job ...*

Write your answers on your notepad, and keep writing until your Inner Witness has run out of things to say.

Circle the responses that make sense to you and examine them. Which of the five practices do you need to work the most? Are some of your fears caused by remembering the past or anticipating the future? ("Shaky," "afraid they'll say no," and "afraid of what they'll think of me" in the previous example.) If so, re-read chapter 4 on living in the present and use the thought-stopping exercise (exercise 23) further on in this chapter.

Are some of your answers related to trust? ("Afraid they'll say no" and "I could end up fired, with no job" in the previous example.) If so, use the alternate nostril breathing or the three-phase breathing exercise (exercises 13 and 15), whichever is your favorite, from chapter 6. Once you've gotten into the rhythm of the breath, tell yourself with every inhale, "I'm safe." You'll need to practice the breathing exercises regularly, preferably daily, so you can really embody the trust that comes from oneness. Call on your support network and ask for help with practical tasks. In the previous example, friends could help with writing a proposal for a pay raise.

RECOGNIZING FEAR

Fear isn't just about fear of change. Fear shows up in life in an infinite number of ways that block us from living our lives to the fullest and experiencing the joy that comes from oneness. Let's take a closer look at the wider world of fear, beginning with how to recognize it.

Most women I know don't wander into dangerous neighborhoods alone, don't hitchhike by themselves, don't stray too far from home unaccompanied after dark. I've never felt that kind of fear. I've been lost in Washington, DC, late at night without a map, searching for a youth hostel. I've strayed into San Francisco's Tenderloin unscathed and hitchhiked through New England alone. But the night I was asked to cover a business association meeting for a small local newspaper, I couldn't make myself open the door to the meeting room and step inside. My hand grasped the door handle, but I couldn't make myself turn it. I walked away, came back, tried again, walked away again. After the third attempt, I stayed away. I've never feared being attacked by people, but I've been petrified of talking to them, and it showed in my inability to open a door and walk on through it.

Fear comes in varying degrees of intensity. Extreme fear is a powerful, icy hand with a vise grip on our guts. We feel it in our stomach as nausea and in our intestines as the kind of muscle contractions that send us running to the toilet. Or it leaves us gasping for air in the middle of a panic attack.

Extreme fear is a response to a perceived imminent threat. That threat may be real or imagined. I've known people for whom leaving the house was a heroic struggle they had to push themselves through every single day, and for no obvious reason. To an outside observer, their lives were not exceptionally stressful. They faced no threat, not even a risk. But on the inside, everything appeared threatening. In traffic, the driver of the car behind seemed menacing, someone walking along the street could be a mugger, a dog barking in a yard could be savage. Extreme fear paralyzes the spirit. A life lived in fear is often barely recognizable as a life at all.

While fear of imminent threat is felt in the abdomen, fear of what might possibly/probably happen sometime in the future is located higher up in the body. This type of fear creates queasiness in the stomach, fluttering in the chest, stiff alertness, and an obsessive, racing mind. These are the symptoms of anxiety.

The Second Practice: Living in the Present. The most pernicious aspect of anxiety is the rapid flow of thoughts. The mind focuses obsessively on what might happen and how terrible that will surely be. It runs through scenarios, most of which end badly. These thoughts have an instant effect on the body, which is where emotions are felt. Daniel Goleman, in his book *Emotional Intelligence,* gives a detailed and arresting account of the physiological changes triggered in the body by a single fearful thought. People with chronic anxiety experience this pent-up tension every day. Not surprisingly, it leads to all sorts of health issues, from depression to stomach problems to hypertension.

People who suffer from anxiety can spend a lot of time focused on the future. The second practice, Living in the Present, is vital for managing the racing mind that feeds anxiety. In the present, there is no anticipation of disaster, nothing to worry about, nothing to fret over. There is only now, and now brings blessed relief from torturous ruminations about the future. Here are three ways to help calm a racing mind and bring us into the anxiety-free present moment.

EXERCISE 23: THOUGHT-STOPPING

a) If you're feeling anxious, write down your thoughts. Let them flow uncensored onto the page. Then read them aloud. Do they sound even a little bit over the top, out of proportion to the situation? Can you laugh at some of them? Can you share them with a friend who can joke about them with you? Humor can put catastrophic thoughts in their place.

b) Use the meditation to silence the chatter (exercise 4) from chapter 4. If you'd like, place a candle before you and keep your eyes open. Whether your eyes are open or closed, focus your attention on your breathing without changing its volume or pace. Follow your inhale and exhale until your mind calms. When thoughts come, visualize them floating away on a river or evaporating in the heat of the candle flame. More thoughts will come; just let them float away.

c) Use the anchoring meditation (exercise 5) from chapter 4 or the alternate nostril breathing or the three-phase breathing exercise (exercises 13 and 15) from chapter 6 to calm your mind. If you are chronically anxious, you will need to use these exercises every day, sometimes several times a day. Make them a priority in your life; otherwise you can slip back into anxiety.

Normal Fear

Between gut-wrenching panic and chronic anxiety lies the fear most people experience at some point in their lives, the kind of fear we regard as normal. "Normal" fear is triggered by an event as opposed to a perceived threat. Common fear-inducing events include interviews, exams, traveling alone to a new place or country, a first date, and public speaking. Because these fears are considered normal, people plow through and do what has to be done. In some cases— during an exam, for example—low-level fear can sharpen performance. But if the fear is strong enough, it can cause us to blank out during the exam. Fear can also stop us from making a speech, taking a trip, or going on that first date.

Low-level "normal" fear forms the shady background to many people's lives: fear of rejection, fear of abandonment, fear of success or failure, fear of being alone, fear of intimacy, fear of attention or its opposite, oblivion. This type of fear is not always easy for other people to see. Shyness is apparent in children, but in adults it's often so well disguised as either chattiness or haughtiness that it's unrecognizable. Other fears become apparent only when you examine the span of a life. A lifetime of unfulfilled potential can point to fear of success or of failure. A lifetime of short-term relationships isn't always due to the bad luck of never meeting the right person. Sometimes it's the result of a subtle yet crippling fear of deep, long-term connection.

THE FEAR RESPONSE

The Enneagram,[34] an ancient and astonishingly accurate tool of self-awareness, describes people's reaction to fear as either phobic or counterphobic. Nobody is phobic or counterphobic all the time, but we lean toward one or the other response. A phobic method of coping with fear looks like the timidity we usually associate with the emotion. A phobic personality obeys rules. "Don't" is a common term in a phobic's lexicon. "Don't say this ... Don't do that ..." It's a mantra he repeats silently to himself and out loud to his children. A phobic's life is fenced in by doing the right thing, or rather doing the thing that's acceptable to others. That way he avoids both conflict and disapproval, but phobics can't avoid the daily pain of anxiety and worry.

Both phobic and counterphobic people say no a lot. Phobics say it quietly, often through their actions and demeanor rather than their words. Counterphobics say it loudly and quickly, even when they've been invited to do something they will enjoy. Counterphobics test people's motives, a habit that can feel abrasive to others. Counterphobics can also show their fear through aggression. Bullying, for example, is often a counterphobic mask for fear.

On a basic level, fearful people don't trust the world to be on their side, and they don't trust themselves to navigate life unscathed. Fearful people need the support of a safe container. That container could be a group of friends or family or one vital relationship. It could be a religion, a political philosophy, or a gang, or it could be the safety of a routine and circumscribed life. Fearful people may bury themselves in their own home, in books, in hobbies, in their job—anything to protect themselves against the terrifying possibility of something new and therefore threatening. Within the boundaries of a safety zone, fear is held at bay. But so is life. Fear shrinks life down to the people and places that are comfortable. It cuts us off from adventure and opportunity.

And even within the walls of a secure routine, anxiety lurks—Is it really secure? Do they really like me? Will it all just crumble away one of these days? The irony is that fear itself can easily cause the edifice to collapse. Being too timid and fearful to ask difficult questions or challenge patterns in a relationship can contribute to the slow death of that relationship. Being too aggressive and constantly testing the loyalty and motivation of friends can drive those friends away. Fear cuts us off from the experience of oneness, the serenity we feel when we're at one with life even when our life is difficult or troubled. Fear obscures the spiritual truth that all shall be well. This is because in the grip of chronic fear, we tend to trust that emotion as a dependable guide through life.

An Unreliable Guide

When I was a child, I convinced myself that a lion had taken up residence in the bathtub. I was afraid to go to the bathroom by myself because I never knew when the lion was going to come roaring out of the tub and attack me. The notion could have been the product of watching too many nature documentaries on TV, or it could have been a manifestation of deeper, subconscious fears. Either way, no lion ever lurked in my parents' bathroom. But the illusion conjured up by my fear was so real that I checked the tub every time I went into the room, fully expecting to see a lion crouching inside and ready to pounce.

Lisa, one of my earliest clients, had less to fear from imaginary wild animals than from real-life second graders. She had been tall for her age, she explained during her first therapy session, and over-weight. When her father's company transferred him to a town on the other side of the country, Lisa dreaded starting over again in a new school. Her fears came to pass. The children in Lisa's new school teased her to her face and joked about her behind her back. It stayed that way right through to eighth grade.

Forty years later, in another new town, Lisa joined a meetup group, then used every excuse she could think of to avoid going to her first group event. Eventually, her husband bundled her into their car and drove her to the venue. She stayed half an hour. A week later, when she arrived for a breathwork session, Lisa swung between criticizing herself for cowardice and criticizing the members of the meetup group for their hostility and unfriendliness. But as she described what had happened at the meetup, Lisa recognized that the people she'd met had gone out of their way to make her feel at home. During breathwork, Lisa made the connection between her torturous experience that began in second grade and the meetup the previous week.

Fear is a rational and healthy response to real danger. It's a primitive physiological reaction that can serve us well in the face of a real threat, a warning to take action or get hurt. Unfortunately, fear is not good at distinguishing between a real threat and an imagined one. Despite this, we still tend to rely on it as an indicator of reality. If we fear something, it must be real or a real possibility. This is not a fool-proof equation. The thing we fear often doesn't exist until our fear conjures it into existence.

Whether we experience groundless fear consistently or just occa-sionally, we can begin to deal with it by first accepting that fear, rather than the thing we fear, is at the heart of our difficulties. As Franklin Delano Roosevelt so famously put it, "The only thing we have to fear is fear itself—nameless, unreasoning, unjustified terror which paralyzes needed efforts to convert retreat into advance."[35] Abandonment hurts, but fear of abandonment stops us from loving. Rejection hurts, but fear of rejection stops us from reaching out and connecting. Failure hurts, but fear of failure stops us from even trying.

I created the lion in the bathtub out of pure imagination. Even though a group of second graders ostracized Lisa for no good reason, it did not follow that a group of middle-aged adults would do the same thing four decades later. We need to use objective common sense to ascertain whether our fear is justified or not. If it is justified, we need to heed its warning and take action. If it's not justified, we need to delve deeper, examine our fear through the prism of the contemplative mind, and separate the emotion from the thing we fear. We do this through working the first practice, Radical Awareness.

THE FIRST PRACTICE: RADICAL AWARENESS AND FEAR

I once worked with a client named Vivienne who obsessed over the safety of her adult son. If he was a few minutes late home from work, she worried about whether he had been in a car accident or attacked on the street. Instead of enjoying her evenings watching TV or spending time with her other children, Vivienne visualized her son dead on the roadside, his car (which he rarely used) mangled beside him. Vivienne's fears were out of proportion to reality, but the images fear generated in her mind were so vivid and dreadful, she convinced herself tragedy was imminent. Vivienne remained in the grip of fear until she was able to make the vital distinction between fear and the thing she feared.

This is a distinction most of us are not very skilled at making, at least not when we first attempt to put the first practice, Radical Awareness, into action. We move rapidly from fear to the object of our fear so rapidly that we believe the emotion is caused by the thing we are afraid of. The thing we fear may not exist, but focusing on it, rather than on the emotion itself, can reinforce the illusion of its reality. It may even conjure the thing we fear into reality.

Review Excrcise 22: Understanding Fear of Change from earlier in this chapter. You created a list of the things you feared when contemplating making a change in some aspect of your life. The example I used was of someone asking for a raise. One of the fears was getting a "no" response from the boss. A "no" response is a real possibility. But so is a "yes." Given the circle of effect we studied in chapter 7, the fear of getting a "no" could easily be the deciding factor. If an employee approaches his boss while in the grip of fear, his body language, tone of voice, and energy, as well as the quality of his arguments in favor of a raise, will all be affected by the anticipation of failure. He will exude the message that he expects the boss to say no, thus making it easier for the boss to turn down the request. The employee in the grip of fear will also more easily take that "no" for an answer and not argue the point. Fear itself can bring the thing we fear to pass.

In addition, the more real the object of fear becomes, the more it acts as an overflow valve for the emotion. While we obsess about the thing we fear, we can avoid confrontation with fear itself. But when we truly embrace awareness, when we're willing to stand back and objectively scrutinize this tyrant we call fear, we can see the difference between the emotion of fear and the object of our fear. When we recognize this difference and acknowledge the role we play in making our fears come true, we have taken the first major step in the process of overcoming fear.

EXERCISE 24: ISOLATING FEAR

Read your list again from Exercise 22: Understanding Fear of Change. Then very consciously set the list aside. Physically push it to one side just on the edge of your field of vision. Close your eyes and use your favorite breathing technique to anchor yourself in the present. Call in your Inner Witness, and when it is fully present, allow your fear, not what you fear, to take shape before you. Face the emotion. Let it have a color, a texture, a face perhaps. Or let it take the form of a symbol. Observe it for a while and get to know its features. Then, in your own time, let your Inner Witness guide that shape or symbol that represents your fear into a place of quarantine. This could be behind a glass wall where you can see it if you choose to look but it can't reach you. Continue to breathe gently until you get used to the idea that this particular fear is safely locked away in quarantine. Then take a few more deep breaths to complete your meditation. Repeat this exercise any time your fear escapes from quarantine.

GOING DEEPER INTO AWARENESS

Fear of meeting and engaging with people (shyness) is rooted in a deep sense of inadequacy, of not being good enough, interesting enough, entertaining enough. The terror some people experience before making a presentation can be caused by a belief that they should never fail, be less than perfect, appear foolish. Fear of intimacy can be a way of protecting fragile boundaries that could otherwise be breached by the intense closeness of a relationship. The majority of chronic fear is generated by us through our own beliefs. Reaching this belief system is the work of our Inner Witness.

Vivienne used the following starter-sentence writing exercise to allow her Inner Witness to delve deeper into the roots of her fears.

EXERCISE 25: THE ROOTS OF FEAR

Have a pen and paper close at hand. Choose a situation in which you feel fear. Begin with something manageable. The situation you used in Exercise 22: Understanding Fear of Change earlier in this chapter would be good. Close your eyes and begin with five minutes of deep belly breathing. Once you've established your breathing pace and rhythm, bring your fear to mind and hold the situation you've chosen in your awareness. Concentrate on the sensations in your body rather than the thoughts that may be crowding your mind.

When you feel ready, open your eyes and use the following starter sentence to explore the beliefs that underpin your fears. Simply finish the sentence over and over again without thinking. Write down whatever comes to you. Give your Inner Witness complete freedom. Here is how Vivienne completed her sentence:

Starter Sentence: *In this situation, I . . .*

- *I hate when he doesn't come home.*
- *I hate when he doesn't tell me he'll be late.*
- *Why doesn't he tell me? He should call. (She's straying from the assignment here by focusing on her son rather than herself. Her Inner Witness then gently brings her back to "I" sentences.)*
- *I feel awful.*
- *I feel terrible.*
- *I'm going to die.*
- *I can't lose him.*
- *I can't stand it if he dies.*
- *I'll die too.*
- *I die.*

Nothing Vivienne wrote was logical. She wasn't about to die, and although the loss of her son would have felt like a kind of death, she herself would have survived. But the exercise helped her to become aware of the full range of her thoughts and emotions.

Now complete the starter sentence ("In this situation, I…") in relation to your chosen situation of fear. Review your answers. What items resonate the most with you, however illogical they may seem? These may be the roots of your fears. Now that awareness has brought them out into the open, you can begin to address them through meditation, therapy, or conversations with friends and by working the five practices.

As we've seen, the emotion of fear is often bound tightly to the object of our fear. In dealing with a strong emotion, awareness is most effective when focused on the emotion itself as it's felt physically. Bringing awareness to the emotion of fear uncouples the emotion from its object. This can help neutralize the catastrophic thinking that feeds fear. With her worrying mind out of the way and her focus firmly in the present moment, Vivienne, in her Rebirthing breathwork session, had a full-body experience of her own birth during which her heart stopped beating and she came close to death.

If this exercise leads you to beliefs as deep as Vivienne's, you may want to continue your exploration with the support of a breathwork therapist. However, as was the case with Lisa, making the connection between present and past fears may be enough to dissipate your fears. Often awareness alone is enough to remove the barrier between us and the freedom of oneness with ourselves and life. But dealing with fear is often a slower process, a matter of learning to trust ourselves and life, step by step, day by day. This is where the practices of Trust and Oneness come into play.

THE THIRD AND FIFTH PRACTICES: TRUST AND OPENNESS, ONENESS

The object of chronic fear is generally not a life-threatening situation but an ordinary event, a common occurrence in most people's lives. Yet we spend much of our precious time trying to ward off what is a normal life event. We dread the awfulness, the darkness. We hide from life to avoid fear, so fear becomes a barrier between us and full-on living. But when we reach an experience of oneness, we find love. It's impossible to feel fear in the presence of the kind of love that infuses a oneness state, because "perfect love casts out all fear" (1 John 4:18). There is a feeling of being held by life, a feeling that all will be well. Trust opens to oneness, oneness opens us to trust, and trust is the antithesis of fear. When we do experience loss, rejection, and failure, when we experience them fully and with awareness and trust, the quality of our living changes. We engage fully with the rawness and richness of life without the barrier of fear.

These are times when the risk of rejection, of success or failure, of abandonment, or of whatever else we perceive as a threat loses its power over us. This holding of opposites, of paradox, within ourselves is a key to managing fear. We can be aware of fear and be calm at the same time. We can choose to immerse ourselves in calmness just as we can choose to abandon ourselves to fear. It's not that the risk does not exist, but we can manage it. Because we trust the spiritual alchemy that transforms adversity into growth, we know we can survive anything that happens to us.

As we do the work of spiritual growth through radical awareness and the other practices, self-development exercises like the ones in this book, and regular breathwork or meditation, the belief systems at the source of our fear begin to change. Because we no longer feel so inadequate, because it becomes okay to look foolish and be imperfect, because our boundaries are now stronger, fear diminishes. The more we experience being one with life, the closer we get to the plateau state of calm stillness, the less we are visited by fear. I'm still a little stiff when encountering new people, but it's been a very long time since I turned down the opportunity to meet them.

9

STOP THINKING
LIKE A VICTIM

You take your life in your own hands, and what happens?
A terrible thing: no one to blame.

~ERICA JONG

The twins were always the first to arrive. Every Thursday afternoon without fail they shuffled through the doors of the community center training room and commandeered the two armchairs. Although in their late forties, both women looked and dressed much older. Other women in the stress management group I ran struggled with poverty, raising young children, or life in tough Dublin neighborhoods. The twins, Susan and Rita, had none of those problems. Children grown, husbands with professional jobs, mortgages almost paid off, they could have been enjoying life. But they were even more stressed out than the other women in the class.

The twins weren't actually twins, or even sisters. They were life-long friends who had grown so alike over the years that the other women in the group called them the Bobbsey Twins. The name stuck. The twins liked to talk. Over a series of classes, a pattern emerged. The twins would list the apparently endless stream of difficulties they faced. The other women would offer simple, potentially effective solutions. The twins would then come up with reasons those solutions would not work. All of those reasons involved their husbands.

Both women loved gardening. Susan needed to buy a new lawn-mower, but her husband wouldn't cooperate. The old mower was just fine by him. Why should he drag himself away from his Saturday golf game to go shopping for something he didn't need anyway?

"Go by yourself," someone in the group suggested. "You have the money. Go and buy it yourself."

"He won't help me get it out of the car," Susan responded.

"So? Get it delivered," another woman offered. "They'll even take away your old one."

"He'll just complain about it," Susan answered. "He complains about everything. Yesterday he . . ." and she was off, subject changed, solution successfully avoided.

Later in the class, Rita would share a different problem, but the conversation would always follow the same pattern.

The twins had a way of interacting with the world that is often called "victim thinking." In common parlance, a victim is someone who has been hurt by someone or something more powerful than themselves. Victims of car accidents, violence, natural disasters, or swindles all face powerful forces. Not so the victim thinker. Susan and Rita's biggest adversary was their victim mind.

Susan's and Rita's husbands (who were actually brothers) preferred to spend time with their golfing buddies over their wives. The men were annoyingly uncooperative. They grumbled and complained about most things. But the brothers were not aggressive.

Neither sister felt threatened in any way by the men they married. Yet both women acted as if they needed their husband's permission to do almost everything—buy a lawnmower, choose what to cook for dinner, go to the movies, take a vacation. Susan and Rita lived life at half measure. They both longed for more. If only their husbands would cooperate.

The victim mind has a way of approaching life from the position of the underdog. To victim thinkers like Susan and Rita, power lies with other people—in this case, their husbands. In reality, the twins had passed their forty-something years locked inside the prison of their own victim minds, waiting for permission to live, almost completely unaware of the glittering world of freedom that radical awareness could offer them.

ANATOMY OF A VICTIM MIND

Victim thinkers often race in circles, repeating the same behavior over and over again, seeking a different result. A victim thinker's starting point for spiritual and psychological growth is the first practice, Radical Awareness. In my experience, victim thinkers struggle more than most with awareness. Their Inner Witness has long ago faded from sight. So let's begin by becoming aware of how a victim thinker thinks.

Needing Approval: A victim mind needs approval from others. Both Susan and Rita needed their husbands' approval for almost everything, including social activities. The husbands never approved of anything and never socialized outside of weekend golf. The result: because Susan and Rita wouldn't even take each other out to dinner, they rarely got out of the house. At the time I knew them, the stress management group was their only social outlet.

Just after graduation, I taught high school for four of the toughest years of my working life. In my opinion, I was not a good teacher. Part of the reason for my poor performance lay with the education system itself, but part of it lay squarely with me. I wanted my students to like me, to think I was a good teacher. Needing the children you teach to like you is lethal for classroom management. Children pick up on that need the first day the teacher walks into the classroom. The children I taught had the power to make my working life miserable only because I needed their approval. Needing approval gives power to the person whose approval we seek. Sometimes they take full advantage of that power.

Parents who need the approval of their children make inconsistent disciplinarians. They threaten consequences for breaking a rule but don't always follow through with the punishment. Children learn quickly how to exploit that kind of weakness.

Couples can use disapproval as an instrument of control. Because they know each other so intimately, the subtle signs of disapproval—a look, a tone of voice—can be enough to make an approval-seeking partner compliant.

After weeks of futile discussion, some of the women in the stress management group lost patience with the twins. I could see it in the abruptness of their responses to the twins' problems. This happens in families, too. Children can feel suffocated by a victim parent. As children grow, they form lives and relationships of their own, independent of their parents. When the child of a victim parent gets upset over something in their own life, the victim parent can get so emotionally overwrought about it that the child ends up taking care of the parent. This is a heavy burden for a young person to bear. Partners, too, can lose respect for someone who is excessively dependent and doesn't take initiative. The spiritual paradox inherent in victim thinking is that seeking approval often leads directly to disapproval—or worse, contempt. Victim thinkers are often derisively called martyrs.

Powerlessness: I grew up in Ireland before the economic boom that an English banker christened the "Celtic Tiger." Ireland had been a colony of Britain for the best part of eight hundred years.

Historians have written about what happens to a colony after it wins independence, the post-colonial period. The post-colonialism is the victim mind on a national level. Fifty years on from independence, the Ireland I grew up in struggled with a massive case of victim thinking. This showed in the country's economic and social policies, but it also filtered down into the heart of many families.

Barack Obama, in *Dreams from My Father*, talked about the Big Man in his father's Kenya. I remember my mother using the very same phrase. The Big Man was anyone a step above us on the economic and social ladder. They had power we couldn't even aspire to, so why bother. Jobs like medicine and law, vacations abroad, writing books, were for the Big Man, not us. We knew our place and trimmed our dreams accordingly. This is power unclaimed, power given away, and it's the defining characteristic of the victim mind.

Victim thinkers assume the position of the powerless in any given situation. Their powerlessness shows in phrases like "They won't...," "He will never...," and "I can't do anything because she..." In the victim mind, the other person has the power. If the victim thinker can't accomplish something, it's because someone else stands in the way. The obstacles may be real, but instead of continuing with dogged persistence, the victim gives up and sinks into powerlessness. Eventually, a victim thinker can get to the point where they take powerlessness for granted and act that way. This can trigger the circle of effect, which means others can treat the victim thinker as if she really doesn't have any power.

A victim depends, to varying degrees, on the permission and approval and sometimes companionship of others. This powerless dependence makes for a restricted, lonely, half-lived life, cut off from the joyful connection with self and life that is oneness.

Control: The victim mind can develop in infancy. Babyhood is a state of powerlessness and dependence. Most babies find ways to get their needs met—they cry, smile, gurgle, and interact in their own way with the adults in their lives. Babies find their power and ask for what they want. But if the baby's needs consistently go unmet, the infant can experience powerlessness.

As we grow, powerlessness comes in other forms. Some children are abused. Others, to varying degrees, learn that they're not attractive, worthy, or lovable. These messages come through parents, family, or even through other children. And we all absorb messages from our culture. Not too many years ago, girls were given the clear message that their happiness and social acceptability depended on snagging a husband.

Wherever the lessons come from, human beings find it difficult to live in complete powerlessness. The victim is driven to snatch back some shred of power for themselves. The power of the victim lies in control. Some of the methods victim thinkers use to control others include:

- **Neediness:** Acting helpless, crying during conflict, seeking approval before acting or making decisions, seeking a companion for new ventures instead of proceeding alone.
- **Fixing:** Trying to solve other people's problems for them, smoothing out conflicts, backing down from anger, anticipating what others will think, taking cues from other people about how to behave.
- **Overworking:** Saying yes to work both in the workplace and at home, even to the point of exhaustion.
- **Pleasing:** Doing what other people want, anticipating the needs of others, being overly compliant.
- **Manipulating:** Maneuvering and strategizing.

People who use these strategies are not easy to live with, so it's easy to feel resentment toward them. But the only way victims know how to win and keep love is to bind others to themselves through guilt and manipulation. No matter how irritating or suffocating their strategies are to others, the victim is driven by the deep pain of feeling less than adequate, lovable, or wanted.

Loss of Self: Toward the middle of the stress management course, Rita told the group that she had decided to redesign her garden. Several times she asked her husband what flowers and plants he'd like in the garden. True to form, he didn't care. Because he wouldn't tell Rita what color he wanted, Rita couldn't redesign.

"Pick your own plants," the woman sitting next to her said.

The others joined in and demanded to know why she didn't just buy plants and get on with the job. Rita broke down. Her crying began as a way of getting the rest of the group to feel sorry for her, thereby keeping them off the topic. But this time the group would not be moved. They asked more questions. Rita made some half-hearted excuses for not buying what she wanted for the garden. But under pressure from the other women, Rita stepped out from behind her victim mask. And she stepped right into the genuine pain that lurks beneath victim thinking. Then the real story emerged.

Rita had, in fact, anticipated the group's advice. She and Susan had gone to a garden center together to choose Rita's favorite plants. But Rita didn't know what her favorite plants were. She stood in the flowering perennial section of the center, surrounded by plants, paralyzed. Then the two women left the garden center empty-handed, Rita crying uncontrollably.

In the middle of the garden center, Rita came face to face with the tragedy of the victim mind. She no longer knew what she liked or didn't like. Victims spend so much time thinking about other people and how to please them and are so focused on being powerless that they lose contact with themselves. They lose sight of something as fundamental as their preference in flowers. The loss of self leaves a spiritual vacuum at the core of the victim thinker. This vacuum is a recipe for stress, addiction, and loneliness. It's a breeding ground for codependent and abusive relationships.

Disowning Responsibility: Sometimes when a child falls and hurts himself, his parent may slap the thing the child fell against and say, "Bad chair" (or floor, or table, or whatever the object happens to be). This way of helping a child deal with the shock and sometimes embarrassment of falling is, in itself, harmless. But within it lies the dynamic of the victim mind: disowning responsibility. "Powerful chair hurt powerless me. I have no responsibility for walking into it instead of around it." It's an early, well-meaning lesson in how to think like a victim.

Nobody doubted the fact that Susan's and Rita's husbands were chronic complainers with little or no interest in their wives. Nobody in the group wanted to swap marriages with the twins. But the twins knew what they needed to do to create a better life. They needed to go out and buy a lawn mower, redesign the garden, and go on vacation together. Yet instead of taking action, they blamed their husbands. Blame is often a sign that we are disowning responsibility for aspects of our lives. The twins disowned responsibility for their own happiness.

Taking responsibility means we recognize and accept the role we play in shaping our own life. If we've grown up thinking like a victim, this kind of responsibility can seem incomprehensible. But it's an important concept to grasp, because responsibility equals power. When we disown responsibility, we give our power away and leave our happiness dependent on others.

Rita and Susan blamed their husbands for the fact that they hadn't been on vacation—in Rita's case in over ten years, in Susan's, almost five. But Rita and Susan could have gone on vacation without their husbands. They chose not to. Then they disowned responsibility for that choice by blaming it on their husbands. While they disowned responsibility for their choices, nothing changed in the twins' lives. Summers passed with nothing more than a few day trips to golf tournaments. But once the twins acknowledged their responsibility, summers shimmered with possibility. They began to plan a vacation in Italy, and as far as I know, they took that vacation with each other.

VICTIM MIND—CONTEMPLATIVE MIND

The First Practice: Radical Awareness: All five practices have relevance to the victim thinker, but more than anything else, a victim thinker needs a particularly vigilant Inner Witness. The victim's mind runs a complex network of control and avoidance strategies. Because these strategies have become second nature to the victim, the convoluted twists and turns of her own mind are exceptionally difficult for the victim to spot. It took months for Susan and Rita to recognize what the other women in the group saw immediately—the twins' endless stream of excuses for inaction.

A victim's Inner Witness needs to look out for the phrase "I can't" in all its forms:

- She won't let me.
- It wouldn't work.
- It doesn't matter anyway.
- I don't mind.
- Yes, but …
- Whatever you want.
- Whatever. (Said with a shrug, in a tired tone of voice.)
- It is what it is. (Said with resignation.)

"I can't" signals a lack of power. The simple practice of changing "I can't" to "I won't" has a powerful effect. "I won't" signals ownership and responsibility. The feeling of personal power resonates throughout the body. Over time, a victim thinker who has committed herself to the path of awareness will learn to recognize the physical sensations of power and responsibility. She'll stand straighter, feel stronger, and breathe more freely.

The Fifth Practice: Oneness: The other important practice for victim thinkers is the experience of mystical love, or oneness. People naturally seek love from partners, family, and friends. Most of us look to others every day for the warmth of their good will and caring. But for a victim thinker, this is a desperate kind of seeking. Rita, in particular, longed for affection from her husband. She craved kind words and bent herself out of shape to please him.

"I thought he'd love me more if I agreed with him about everything," she explained to the stress management group. "He liked being the one who knows what to do. He liked it when I couldn't do things. I didn't see it happening, but I forgot how to do things."

The twins scrambled after any scraps of praise or kindness that came their way. Always looking outward, they never thought that love could come from inside themselves. The victim thinker hasn't experienced mystical love, that matrix of unconditional, unearned love we find in states of oneness. Because they don't know mystical love, victims believe their only source of love is outside of themselves. And because they've never known unconditional, abundant love, victims believe love must be earned, always. The root of victim thinking lies in this separation from love.

Mystical love doesn't depend on whether we think we're lovable or unlovable, pleasing to others or not. Mystical love doesn't have to be earned or controlled or clung to with desperation. Mystical love doesn't go away. This unconditional, steadfast love is the perfect antidote to a victim's crippling sense of inadequacy. As the poet Rumi put it, "When the soul lies down in that grass, the world is too full to talk about."[36] In this state, it's impossible to be a victim thinker, because in a state of oneness, separation doesn't exist.

On the journey from victimhood to autonomy, the victim must face responsibility. She must face the fact that often the limits we believe others set for us are, in fact, the limits we set for ourselves. The victim learns to trust love, to trust that she is loved without condition. This trust, at one point, would have been too frightening to even contemplate. Now, for a victim, it's the point at which adventures begin. The following exercises can help turn a victim mind into a contemplative mind.

EXERCISE 26: DO I NEED APPROVAL?

Take a notepad and pen and answer the following questions. Keep writing until you run out of answers:

- When someone praises me, I feel ...
- When someone disapproves of me or something I've said or done, I feel ...

If you have anything stronger than a mild emotional and/ or physical reaction to either approval or disapproval, your need for approval may be greater than is healthy. In situations where you have a strong emotional reaction to disapproval, take the time to do some slow belly breathing. Then visualize your Inner Witness giving you a warm hug and telling you that you are loved and accepted just as you are.

EXERCISE 27: MY RELATIONSHIP TO POWER

Pick a situation in which you feel your hands are tied, that right now there's nothing you can do to change things. Your hands may well be tied, but that doesn't mean you have to think like a victim. Use the twenty connected breaths (exercise 12) from chapter 6, and when your breathing rhythm is established, bring this situation to your awareness. Hold it before you and let your Inner Witness take over. Let your Inner Witness point out where your personal power lies. It could lie anywhere: in acceptance, walking away, speaking out, forgiveness, confrontation, finding an alternative, or something entirely different. For example, power for the twins lay in accepting their husbands for who they are. Once the twins accepted the reality of the men they married, the women could begin to meet each other's needs for companionship. In acceptance they found power and freedom.

EXERCISE 28: RECLAIMING POWER

Whenever you find yourself saying "I can't" in any of its forms, replace it with "I won't." Observe how that feels physically and emotionally. That is what personal power feels like. Then think about decisions you have to make, small decisions like where to go for dinner with friends or what color to paint your front door. If you have a tendency to hold back your opinion and go along with what others want, try figuring out what you really do want. You don't have to voice your preference to anyone but yourself if you don't want to. But make a choice and see how that feels emotionally and physically. Then you can choose whether you want to verbalize your preferences to others or not. Your power lies in having a choice.

EXERCISE 29: CONNECTING WITH LOVE

Practice the anchoring meditation (exercise 5) from chapter 4. When you get to the feeling of pleasure and contentment, start telling yourself "I am loved" in rhythm with your inhale. It doesn't matter who or what loves you. Spiritual love is a state of being. Then let the phrase gently pass away into silence, and experience the pleasure of connection with yourself. Practice this meditation daily.

10

BREAKING THE BONDS OF ANGER

*Holding on to anger [is like] grasping a hot coal
with the intent of throwing it at someone else.
You, of course, are the one who gets burned.*
~JOAN BORYSENKO, PhD,
MINDING THE BODY, MENDING THE MIND

After my first year in college, I spent the summer juggling three wait-ressing jobs in a coastal town. Woolworth's cafeteria was easy. I kept the self-service counter stocked, brought the odd special order out to the tables, and indulged my creativity by flinging strawberries at the fruit displays. It was a pleasant, relaxed place to work. Sunday morn-ing in the fifty-seater steak and eggs place across the street from the Catholic church was a different story.

No sooner had the crowd from one Sunday mass paid their bills at the Egg House and slid their tips under their dirty plates than another Mass let out. Wave after wave of hungry parishioners filled the tables, and everyone wanted eggs. Eggs came with toast, but the revolving industrial toaster couldn't keep up with demand. The faster the service, the bigger the tip, so waitresses stole each other's toast—until the morning the waitress in the white stocking boots picked up an enormous carving knife and flung it at the waitress with the red wig. The cleaver missed her ear by inches. Red Wig dropped the evidence—a rather large pile of toast—and ran screaming for the restaurant owner. I never saw her again.

This was the first time I'd ever seen anger erupt into violence. I'd seen people get snappy before, usually under the pressure of work, or children who wouldn't behave, or the frustration of not having enough money to pay the bills. But wielding a carving knife over a few slices of toast? I felt above it all, a little smug, if truth be told … until my turn came.

I'd become friends with one of the other waitresses, a fellow student. She had to leave town unexpectedly because of a family emergency and forgot to give me her contact details. On one of my rare mornings off, I returned to the restaurant to ask the owner for my friend's home address. It was a Monday, so no mass. The only people in the restaurant were the owner and the white-booted knife thrower, squeezed together into a booth, his big hand covering her left breast.

Up to then, they'd kept their relationship hidden from the staff. I don't know if I embarrassed them by stumbling onto their secret or not, but they both laughed when I asked for my friend's address.

"Ask me nicely," the owner said as he leered and fondled White Boots's other breast.

I asked again. He scribbled something on a napkin and tossed it at me. It fluttered to the floor, landing at my feet. They waited for me to pick it up. My face burned with humiliation, and at that moment my world went black.

I'd always thought "blind rage" was just a figure of speech, a way of describing how anger can blind people to common sense. Picking up the napkin, I discovered that intense anger can literally take away your vision, which was a good thing because my immediate impulse was to pin his hand to her breast with the nearest fork. And over a table napkin?

In that moment I tasted real rage, the kind of anger that makes people do stupid things, things that are the opposite of what is in their best interest. This is the kind of anger that keeps relationships in conflict for decades and often turns to violence, and it's always about a lot more than a plate of toast or a paper napkin. But not all anger is destructive.

USEFUL ANGER

Winston Churchill, a man whose courage helped lead the world through one of the most violent periods in history, saw the positive side of anger. He once wrote that "a man is about as big as the things that make him angry." Anger at injustice, brutality, racism, and inequality can spur people on to social activism. Anger channeled into constructive action can change a life or a nation. When Rosa Parks refused to surrender her seat to a white passenger on a bus in Birmingham, Alabama, she was surely driven by anger as well as weariness and political strategy. Her small, nonviolent act of angry defiance sparked a civil rights movement that changed a nation forever.

The energy of anger can help us take the action needed to set things right in relationships and situations. Anger helps us set boundaries. It tells us when a line has been crossed, when people have taken advantage of us, disrespected or violated us in some way. It can give us the courage to say no, to be assertive, to stand up for ourselves and others. Anger is an essential tool for navigating relationships.

This kind of anger is a healthy, balanced response to something that happens in the world around us, and it is usually in proportion to the event that sparked it. When things have been set right, anger disappears. Under stress, anyone can flare into a blind rage. It's a clear warning that stress levels need attention. But remove the stress, and this anger too subsides. Chronic anger is different.

CHRONIC ANGER

Joan Borysenko spoke about the kind of anger we hold on to, the hot coal that eats away at our body and soul as well as the lives of people who love us. This kind of anger is always there, underpinning every moment. It flares easily and frequently at the smallest of things: a tone of voice, a minor transgression, being asked an innocent question. It can even be ignited by a compliment. It's out of proportion to the events that trigger it and is often destructive. This is called chronic anger, and, as with fear, it can be one of the most formidable barriers between us and the experience of oneness.

Chronic anger can be categorized under two broad headings:

- Covert anger, which is hidden, suppressed, and often "acted in" (turned against the self).

- Overt anger, which is visible and acted out toward others. Overt anger is what we usually think of when we talk about anger.

It's not a hard and fast rule, but men and women experience and express chronic anger differently. Men tend to act out anger, but not always. Male anger can often be *overt*, visible for what it is, sometimes violent.

Although not true for all women, female anger can be *covert*. It can show up as something else—chronic negativity, a refusal to join in with activities, avoidance, bitchiness, manipulation, passivity, or subservience.

Chronic anger, whether overt or covert, is a way of being, a constant companion. It's an angry person's mode of interaction with the world. Chronic anger is an unambiguous signal that something needs to be addressed. The problem is we're not always clear about what exactly that something is or how to address it. And because anger can take many guises, the chronically angry person is often the last one to recognize the signs of their own rage.

RECOGNIZING ANGER—THE BODY SPEAKS

Emotions are felt in the body. Love, for example, is felt as a diffused glow in the chest, and sorrow is a more intense pain in the same location. In the Eastern energy system, this is the heart (or fourth) chakra. In the West, we are heartbroken or heartsick or bighearted. Anger is felt lower down, in the guts and stomach, the lower chakras. We have a fire in our belly, our guts in a twist, our knickers in a knot. Anger can be a burning sensation, an intensity, a coldness.

Anger is part of the body's fight-or-flight response to danger. It makes the fight part possible. When anger is sparked, adrenaline and cortisol course through the body. The adrenaline rush from anger radiates down our arms and legs and up through our chest and neck. It can cause our heart to race and our muscles to tense up. We feel more powerful. We feel ready for action. That's the purpose of healthy anger: to help us take action.

If the fight response is triggered many times a day, as it is with chronic anger, the emotion takes a high toll on the body. Chronic anger brings headaches, muscle tension and pain, high blood pressure, a racing heartbeat—all the health issues that lead to heart attacks, strokes, and other major illnesses.

The devastation that trails in the wake of chronic anger doesn't stop with the body. Even if the angry person does nothing more than sit quietly in a chair, the anger they exude can be felt by the people around them. But angry people generally do more than sit and seethe. They act, and their actions affect the way people respond to them. An angry person often doesn't see the connection between their anger and the shapes and contours of their life, but whether they can see it or not, chronic anger, expressed or denied, contaminates almost every facet of life. This is why chronic anger so thoroughly separates us from the joy and peace of union with ourselves and life.

While overt and covert anger often look very different to an outside observer, they share a common root. All emotions are heavily influenced, perhaps wholly caused, by our beliefs, and none more so than chronic anger. Anger is fueled by the belief that the world is a hostile place. In the life of a chronically angry person, this belief becomes a classic self-fulfilling prophecy.

If we see the world as a hostile place, we believe people will hurt or betray us, given half a chance. How we see determines what we see, so this belief colors our world. Casual comments can become insults, facial expressions become "looks," and conversations we're not part of become conspiracies against us. Even when people are being nice, the chronically angry person distrusts them, questions their honesty, and wonders what they're really up to.

Chronic anger narrows our vision of the world. If someone speaks sharply, a chronically angry person sees it as an attack. This limited perspective does not allow for the possibility that the other person could be tired, stressed out, making a joke, or any other interpretation of their behavior that is not about the angry person. Anger is such a strong emotion that it often overwhelms our awareness. It's difficult for our Inner Witness to see clearly through the fog of anger.

Both overt and covert anger distort our ability to act in our own best interests. Fiery anger makes it hard to listen to words of caution or common sense. Advice can be seen as undermining or attacking. Consequently, the angry person is blind to alternative solutions and is likely to blurt out things best left unsaid, particularly when talking to people who are trying to help them. In contrast, people who suppress anger are often too willing to listen to the opinions of others in preference to their own ideas. It's easy to make poor decisions this way. Acting out rage can be destructive, but the price for ignoring anger can be equally high.

THE FIRST PRACTICE: RADICAL AWARENESS

Because anger blinds, Radical Awareness is probably the most vital, and the most difficult, practice to implement for the angry person. To shed the light of awareness on the many faces of chronic anger, let's look at the lives of two women, one mired in denial of her anger, and one who acted her anger out on the people around her.

Covert Anger—Anger Denied: Donna met her partner Katie when they volunteered together on a campaign to stop the development of a shopping mall in their neighborhood. Katie was confident and assertive and a natural leader. Donna was shy and quiet, but her sharp mind made her a good behind-the-scenes strategist. They worked well together, were attracted to each other, and began a romantic relationship.

From the beginning, Katie had a tendency to talk over Donna at meetings. In therapy, several years later, Donna recalled those meetings and the feeling of tension in her stomach and chest whenever Katie dismissed her ideas in public. But Donna had grown up in a family where only her mother was allowed to show emotion. The particular emotion—anger, joy, sorrow—didn't matter. They all upset her mother. Donna learned quickly to pull her feelings back inside herself.

Donna didn't recognize the feeling in her stomach for what it was. Or more accurately, she had learned to ignore it. She made excuses for Katie's behavior: Katie was a brilliant speaker, so it was more appropriate that she should carry the meetings. Katie was a clearer thinker, so her strategies were more effective. People liked her more than Donna, so Katie made a more effective front person. The list of Katie's virtues was endless.

Donna came to therapy because her relationship with Katie was disintegrating. As they both agreed that Donna was the problem, Katie did not attend sessions. Donna's absentmindedness was a flash point for both of them. She did strange things, like serving food she knew Katie didn't like. On evenings when the women had arranged to go out together after work, Donna would come home just a little late. Or she'd wash Katie's favorite white shirt with something that bled color into the water. Was she suffering from early-onset dementia? Then one afternoon, Donna caught herself in the act. Katie had dropped a necklace on the floor of their bedroom. Donna was vacuuming. She saw the necklace, knew what it was, and sucked it right up into the vacuum cleaner. What's more, she felt good about it. That's when Donna began to recognize her own anger.

An unbalanced relationship like Donna and Katie's, where one person dominates and the other acquiesces, generates natural, healthy anger. If it's not expressed directly and appropriately, anger seeps out from behind the façade of love disguised as something else—in Donna's case, ditzy incompetence. Donna was loving and compliant. She bent and twisted herself to keep Katie happy. At the same time, she just seemed to keep getting things wrong. Coincidentally, the things she got wrong were things that irritated Katie the most. This type of behavior is called passive aggression.

Donna paid the price of ignoring or suppressing her healthy anger at the outset of the relationship. She came to therapy struggling under the weight of a deepening depression. The act of suppressing her anger also played a major role in the disintegration of her relationship with Katie.

Most people have a natural instinct to set boundaries. Anger is one of the warning signals that our boundaries have been breached. When the self-regulating mechanism of anger is ignored or denied, relationships can become unhealthy. Ignoring anger is a feature of many abusive relationships in which the "victim" of the abuse was not able to take a stand on his or her own behalf in the very early days. As time passes, patterns develop that are hard to break, and eventually even hard to see from inside the relationship.

The tension in Donna's stomach during those early meetings with Katie was her own anger. That anger told her that she was not being treated with respect, that she needed to stand up for herself and set healthy limits to the relationship. Instead, Donna ignored her own instincts. She negated herself.

Learning to express anger effectively is a vital interpersonal skill. Anger gone to ground makes it difficult to speak up for yourself appropriately or at all. Faced with conflict, Donna cried. The link between anger and crying can be frustrating, as if wires are crossed somewhere that can't be unscrambled. But crying, at least initially, makes the conflict go away, and that is what a covertly angry person wants most: to make the conflict go away. Making conflict go away and resolving conflict are two different things. The only way to resolve conflict is to express it early and appropriately. It was a skill Donna had yet to learn.

Over time and lots of breathwork, Donna began to speak up for herself. Instead of playing the victim, the helper, the nice girl, she spoke her mind directly. It wasn't well received, and in the end, they both decided to end the relationship. Donna lost Katie, but she gained large parts of herself. A couple of years and a lot of therapy later, she decided that the trade-off was more than worth it.

Are you covertly angry? Here's an exercise to help you practice awareness in relation to hidden anger.

EXERCISE 30: AWARENESS OF COVERT ANGER

Review your relationships with your partner, friends, and family. Then answer the following questions:

- How often do you put the wishes of others before your own desires, needs, or preferences?
- How often do your friends and family do the things you want?
- Is there a balance between the two (sometimes you do what they want, other times they follow your wishes)?

If you regularly put the wishes of others before your own, the next time it happens, take note of how you feel in that moment. Remember Donna's stomach tension early in her relationship with Katie? Do you have any similar physical responses? Do you feel resentment, anger, resignation, or fear? If you experience emotional or physical responses, take note. You may be suppressing your anger.

OVERT ANGER—ANGER ACTED OUT

Unlike the many sublimations and disguises of covert anger, overt anger is clearly visible as aggression. It's common to think of aggression as violence, as physical or sexual abuse. For millions of people around the world, that's exactly what it is. But aggression has many faces, not all of them violent. Louise is good example of someone who expresses nonviolent aggression.

Louise's parents tried to conceive a baby for seven years before they adopted four-year-old Louise. The adoption was her father's idea. He longed to have a big family. As sometimes happens, after the adoption went through, Louise's mother became pregnant. Both parents shifted their focus from Louise to her baby sister and then to the four babies who followed over the next twelve years.

Louise couldn't remember when her mother began to beat her. The beatings started with open-handed slaps on her legs and escalated quickly into whippings with a leather belt. Childhood was a lonely, bleak existence until around age eight, when Louise discovered surrogate parenting. At that time, Louise had two younger sisters, a baby brother, and a mother who never wanted children. Louise began to bathe and feed the three children, change their diapers, and put them to bed at night. Playing mother had distinct advantages. Louise's mother grew to rely on her. The more indispensable she became to her own mother, the longer the interval grew between beatings. That alone transformed the quality of her life. But what really changed things for Louise was that this lonely girl now had three—and eventually five—adoring little people who clung to her, depended on her, and loved her. She embraced surrogate motherhood with desperation and willingly sacrificed large parts of herself to do so.

Instead of resorting to childish tantrums and teenage rebellion—the normal expressions of anger—Louise became responsible and reliable. Instead of staying out late with friends, she cooked for the family and cleaned house. She rarely dated, and when her younger sisters and brother grew up and moved out of the family home, she found a replacement in her aging parents. By her early forties, Louise's life revolved around her parents. She drove them wherever they wanted to go, even though they could have easily driven themselves. She cut up the food on their plates when they could still feed themselves. This profound level of self-sacrifice often generates a seething resentment, and sooner or later revenge is exacted. Louise began to calculate the price her siblings would pay for the care she lavished on their parents.

Louise came to therapy for depression. She blamed it on the stress of caring for her parents and her no-good sisters and brother. In her own mind, she was a caring, loving daughter who shouldered the entire burden of her elderly parents alone. When we began to focus on her family situation, a different pictured emerged. Her anger was seeping out in nasty ways.

Louise had developed a habit of making appointments for family occasions and then lying about dates and times and locations. Her brother missed their parents' fiftieth wedding anniversary. He arrived on time at the restaurant where Louise told him the celebration would be held. Meanwhile, five miles away, his family sat down to dinner without him in the restaurant Louise had actually booked. Louise explained this away by saying that if he really cared about his parents, he would have double-checked the location. One of Louise's sisters invited their parents to stay with her on weekends to give Louise a break. Louise decided that her sister's house wasn't elder-friendly and turned down the offer on behalf of her parents.

To Louise, this was all very logical and reasonable, and she spoke of it in a calm, stoic, long-suffering way. Unlike Donna, who had twisted and contorted herself to meet Katie's requirements, Louise's big stumbling block was that she believed everyone else was wrong and she was right. That's a tough job for any Inner Witness to take on.

Louise never raised her voice to anyone, never hit anyone, and never damaged property. Lots of aggressive people never resort to violence, but they find many other ways to express anger. Perfectionism is a common feature of overt anger. Perfectionists like things done right, and people who don't share their passion for perfection seem flawed. Overtly angry people tend to make rules they expect their family to obey. They often neglect to tell the family about the rules, but that doesn't stop them from flaring into anger when the rules are broken. They may shout and lash out, but if they're good enough at exuding menace, a look is all that's needed to terrorize their family.

As a result, partners and children can become hypervigilant and flinching, apologize a lot, or try so hard to please that they seem insincere. In a way, they are insincere because their motivation is to avoid conflict. This annoys the angry person even more. There is no way for the family to win in this situation. The internal logic of anger turns praise into condemnation, disagreement into criticism, and simple questions into accusations. This way of thinking is too convoluted and obscure for others to chart a steady and safe course though the relationship.

Where violence and severe mental and emotional abuse are involved, sometimes the only safe way is out, but even that is not always safe. A violently angry person is at his most vulnerable, and
often most dangerous, when the family he has consistently abused is
walking away from him.

Many overtly angry people, particularly men, have difficulty with
authority and with rules and regulations. They "buck" the system. The
boss is often a "jerk," and there can be an uneasy tension in the workplace. Tension escalates if the angry employee can't compromise or
change his mind. If a person can't admit, even to themselves, that
they're sometimes wrong, they will head down the wrong path. As a
result, angry people may get passed over for promotions or raises.

EXERCISE 31: AWARENESS AND OVERT ANGER

Re-read the previous section, "Overt Anger—Anger Acted
Out." Put a checkmark next to any of the characteristics of a
person who is overtly angry that apply to you or your life. For
example, do you find yourself thinking people are jerks a lot?
Do you have a set of rules in your home that everyone must
abide by? You may be tempted to say something like, "A lot of
people are jerks," or "It's good to have rules—they keep things
running smoothly." These can be justifications for your own
anger. Leave them aside for now and continue checking the
characteristics that apply to you. If three or four apply, perhaps it's time to take a detached, Inner Witness look at your
own levels of anger.

THE FIRST PRACTICE: RADICAL AWARENESS

Chronically angry people see the world as a hostile place. This belief
is reinforced by the angry person's compulsion to blame. Overtly
angry people often blame openly: "It's their fault." "They made me
do it." "They're wrong, stupid, a moron." With covert anger, blame is

more subtle. It comes out as "I was only trying to help," "What did I do wrong?," or "Why did he/she do this to me?" Blame is insidious. It prevents the angry person from recognizing and taking responsibility for their own anger. But recognizing and taking responsibility are the keys to shaking off the monster that is chronic anger.

Angry people are often hyper-alert and focused on the world around them, but much of what they see is skewed by their own distorted thinking. The Inner Witness can turn this skill of alert observation to advantage by focusing it inward. If you have taken the first step—recognized your own anger—then your Inner Witness has sprung to life and is poised and waiting to go deeper. The second step is taking responsibility.

Let's go back to Donna and Katie. The vacuum cleaner incident woke Donna up to her responsibility for her own anger. When Katie humiliated Donna in public, instead of speaking up for herself, Donna covered her embarrassment with jokes and excuses. Every time she did that, Donna abdicated responsibility for herself. She abandoned herself. The more she abandoned herself, the more she allowed and even fed the dynamic between herself and Katie. This level of awareness (in retrospect) is the work of a strong Inner Witness.

For the angry person, taking responsibility is not easy. Chronically angry people can be critical of others, but they're even more critical of themselves. Self-condemnation is a form of blame turned inward. It can be just as big a barrier to taking responsibility for our anger as blaming others. In contrast, our Inner Witness simply observes, and the fact that it does not judge invites us to achieve ever deeper levels of awareness, where responsibility lies.

EXERCISE 32: TAKING RESPONSIBILITY FOR ANGER

If the previous two exercises in this chapter indicate that you have at least some covert or overt anger (chronic or out of proportion to the events that spark it), then complete this exercise. You will need a pen and paper.

Recall your most recent experience of anger, whether expressed at the time or not. Write a brief description of the event in your notepad. Here's an example of both overt and covert anger:

> **Lydia (Overt Anger):** *The living room was a mess when I came home from work, so I yelled at the kids to clean it up.*
>
> **Bev (Covert Anger):** *My husband wanted to watch football on TV for the fifth night in a row. I just left the room and started putting dishes in the dishwasher. I ignored him when he asked me not to turn on the washer until after the game because of the noise it makes.*

Now take some deep breaths and let your thoughts flow freely around the question "Who am I angry with and why?" Write your responses in your notepad. Let the words flow uncensored until there is nothing more to write. Here are the answers Lydia and Bev gave:

> **Lydia (Overt Anger):** *I'm angry with the kids. They don't seem to care how tired I am. And my husband gets home before me. Why can't he tidy up? No, he just sits down and plays with the kids and then I come in and I have to act the heavy with them. It's not fair.*
>
> **Bev (Covert Anger):** *I'm angry with my husband. He gets his own way all the time. He hogs the TV. It never occurs to him that I might want to watch something besides football. Then he yells at me because I'm cleaning up, something he doesn't ever think to do.*

You've just written down who you're angry with and why. Now go back to your favorite breathing exercise from chapter 6. Practice it for about five minutes until any anger that might have arisen as a result of the writing you just did subsides and you feel anchored in yourself and reasonably detached. Invite your Inner Witness to review what you just wrote. Could you have handled the situation more directly? More constructively? If you were to take responsibility for your own anger and try to find a solution to the problem, what could you do differently? Here are Lydia's and Bev's answers:

> **Lydia (Overt Anger):** *I could negotiate with my husband and kids about when they clean the living room and ease off on needing it to be perfect before I get home. I could let them have their play time as long as they clean up afterward.*

> **Bev (Covert Anger):** *I could tell him I can't stand watching football every night. I could tell him what I want to watch sometimes instead of waiting for him to ask me or notice me. Maybe he thinks I'm okay with football or maybe he doesn't think at all.*

The Third and Fourth Practices: Trust and Openness, Growing from Adversity

Anger is a surface emotion, a mask for much deeper feelings and beliefs. If we are to effectively bring awareness to anger, we need to dive beneath its surface and explore. The answer varies with the individual, but the feelings that lie beneath the surface of anger include vulnerability, shame, humiliation, fear, powerlessness, and worthlessness. Anger, with its rush of adrenaline-fueled power, is often the only barrier between the angry person and this cauldron of painful emotions. It's no wonder a chronically angry person tries to hold their world together through aggression, as in Louise's case, or through helping and loving, as with Donna.

The third practice, Trust and Openness, is what makes the dive beneath the surface of anger possible. But it doesn't have to be a full-scale, high-board dive. Our Inner Witness can move with exquisite slowness, testing the waters a little at a time.

Donna had a skillful Inner Witness who knew that anger was going to be the easiest thing for Donna to face. So anger at Katie surfaced first. Then came memories of Donna's mother. These were more disturbing, particularly a memory of her mother towering over her, yelling at little Donna. This unleashed a flood of no-holds-barred anger at her mother, who had died five years previously.

Donna brought photos of her mother to her next Rebirthing breathwork session. The woman was beautiful—voluptuous, radiant, sensual. Donna had inherited her mother's pretty face, but that was where the resemblance ended. Donna's hairstyle, her posture, and her fade-into-the-background clothes made her almost invisible to both women and men. To please her mother, Donna has suppressed a lot more than her anger. She had suppressed her own sexuality, her identity as a woman.

During breathwork, she reached a new level of trust. Trust released an astonishingly intense feeling of jealousy toward her mother. Donna had never consciously felt jealous of anyone in her life. The emotion shocked her. But when we trust our breath, it takes us through the darkness, and darkness is where new life is incubated.

Donna's jealousy was followed by one of the most heartfelt experiences of loss I've witnessed as a therapist. Our sexuality is a fundamental part of who we are. While still a young girl, Donna had lost a major part of herself. That realization of loss unleashed a flood of grief. Donna had done enough breathwork to know the drill—trust and breathe, trust and breathe. She breathed through waves of grief until the session reached its climax, then fell into the bliss of oneness.

In the state of oneness, after the darkness of grief, Donna found spiritual love.

Spiritual love is a state of being in which our virtues and faults, our gender, history, personality, or appearance, have no relevance. We are loved. Period. There is no more soothing balm to the angry soul than unconditional love. There is no more effective way to calm turbulent rage than to experience the bliss of being one with the benevolent, supportive life force. After that session, Donna went shopping for new clothes.

EXERCISE 33: GOING BENEATH YOUR ANGER

If you want to take a dive beneath the surface of your anger, begin with a situation you find relatively easy to deal with. Get a notepad and pen and then write down this variation on the starter-sentence exercise (exercise 25) from chapter 8: "When I'm angry at (person's name), I feel..."

Complete the sentence over and over again until there are no more responses left to write. Here's an example:

"When I'm angry at John, I feel..."

- I feel furious.
- I feel like my arms want to hit something.
- I feel like I can't get him to listen.
- I feel like nobody's listening to me.
- I feel like I can't get anything I want.
- I feel like nobody ever listens to me.

When you've finished, review your answers. Which ones resonate with you as the true cause of your anger? If you experience strong emotions as a result of this exercise, practice the alternate nostril breathing (exercise 13) from chapter 6 or the anchoring meditation (exercise 5) from chapter 4 to get you through the feelings you might otherwise hide from behind a wall of anger.

BE GENTLE

For some people, anger can be a deeply rooted, destructive response to life. The energy of anger is powerful and, after the adrenaline rush has subsided, can be exhausting. Anger can be a difficult emotion to work with therapeutically. If you think chronic anger is ruining your relationships and your enjoyment of living, you may need to work with an experienced therapist or breathworker. These exercises are only the starting point.

The path through anger is rarely straightforward. It meanders, diverts, and frequently doubles back on itself. It requires not just awareness, but practice. It's natural to fall back into old ways of thinking. Under pressure, it's natural to fall back on the default response of anger and blame. This can feel like all the gains have been lost, but they haven't. It's just a lapse, a temporary setback. In the same way our Inner Witness can allow thoughts to float across our mind in meditation or breathwork, witness this lapse for what it is and gently move on. The rewards of awareness and trust are no less than a lifetime of freedom from the scourge of chronic anger.

11

ROLES AND IMAGES:
Freedom from the Expectations of Others

It's your destiny to play an infinity of roles,
but these roles are not yourself.
~DEEPAK CHOPRA, *POWER, FREEDOM, AND GRACE*

In the 1840s, Alexandre Dumas wrote *The Vicomte de Bragelonne*, the final installment of his *Three Musketeers* saga. The book was based loosely on the legendary Eustache Dauger, who spent thirty-four years in French prisons, including the infamous Bastille. Dauger's and Dumas's story became known as *The Man in the Iron Mask*. In 1939 it was first made into a movie, and somewhere around 1965 I saw it on TV. I've never forgotten it.

The mask in question was like no mask I'd ever seen. It closed around the prisoner, encasing his whole head from the base of the neck up, and was locked in place by his jailer. The effect was visceral. I could feel the prisoner's suffocation, feel the horror of having my head encased in iron, possibly for life. The man in the mask could see the world outside his tailor-made jail. He could walk around, talk, read, and dress himself. But he was powerless to free himself from the mask. The image comes back to me every so often. It looms largest when I'm working with someone who feels imprisoned in a role.

What's a role?

A role is a part we play in a group of people. The group can be as small as two people or as large as a nation. It can be a family, a team, a business, a gang, a circle of friends, or any collection of people who come together on a regular basis, either formally or informally.

Groups are formed to accomplish a task: raise children, win a game, make a profit, organize the members' social life. The members of the group take on roles related to the group task, and every group needs a leader. In business, the leader may be called the chief executive officer. In a sports team, the leader often has the title of captain. In a group of friends, the leader won't have a title at all, but regardless of the title, a leader inspires, encourages, and provides vision for the rest of the group members.

Another group member will organize the task. This person appoints, supervises, and supports other members of the group in carrying out their assigned portion of the task. In business, the task organizer is called a manager. In a family, the role is usually filled by parents.

Roles and Systems

Getting the job done, the task accomplished, is the visible face of group life. But behind this façade of work, a fascinating, intricate, and sometimes messy web of interpersonal relationships forms. This web of relationships transforms a collection of individuals into a "group," and the patterns by which they interact become a "system." This is where things get complicated. Like the task, this system too has roles associated with it, and task and system roles can overlap. The purpose of roles is to keep the system going, to protect and develop it. It matters little whether the system is healthy or unhealthy. The function of roles is to maintain the system's existence.

We all play roles. There's no way to avoid playing a role, and nothing inherently wrong with it. In healthy groups, roles are flexible. They're discussed openly. Roles shift and bend, and people move in and out of them. The reason the group was formed, the task, is always in sight, and when all the group members play their roles, the task is accomplished effectively and efficiently.

In an unhealthy system, the opposite is true. The web of relationships can develop without the group realizing the system is forming. As a result, roles emerge unconsciously, and members can take on roles without knowing that's what they're doing. Roles can become fixed and rigid and sometimes impossible to move out of.

Unhealthy groups tend to become defensive when questioned or threatened. The classic example is when one member of a troubled family tries to speak out about abuse within the family. Other family members often close ranks, and the whistleblower is ostracized. In unhealthy groups, preserving the group system takes precedence over the relieving the anguish of any of its members. Preserving the system also takes priority over accomplishing the task.

There is an element of mystery to why we play the roles that we do in any system. In part, the group assigns us a role, and in part, we carve out that role for ourselves, perhaps because we're comfortable with it. Or the role may help us feel that we have value in the group, something to contribute. We may have played a similar role in our family.

Roles emerge to meet the emerging needs of the system. As the role emerges, someone in the group steps forward to play that role.

In healthy groups, this process of developing a role and finding someone to take it on is clearly defined and often documented in minutes. In other groups, it happens unconsciously. The synchronicity involved in this process of matching role to person is fascinating and, in unhealthy systems, almost completely unconscious.

Types of Roles

Roles have many names and infinite variations. The following is a brief list of some of the most visible roles people play in systems, as well as a description of the effect playing that role can have on people who feel trapped within it. These are generalized descriptions. Every aspect of the role described here may not hold true in every instance. The list is by no means exhaustive.

Clown/Joker

The Joker is the entertainer in a group, the one who makes people laugh, who is always ready for a good time. The Joker adds fun and life to a group and can lift people's spirits when things get tough or dull. An unhealthy group can use the Joker to avoid looking at the darker side of their system.

The Downside: Jokers can find it hard to relate to others on a deeper level or to show the darker emotions such as sorrow, anger, or depression. While the Joker can be surrounded by people attracted to her humor, she may have few truly intimate friendships. The mask of the jolly, fun-loving Joker can be far from the truth of the person who feels trapped inside that role.

Rebel

Rebels defy acceptable codes of behavior and values of a group. In a family, teenagers often take on the rebel role and push their parents' boundaries. The Rebel can be the most honest member of the group, and in the process of rebelling, can expose group secrets. If the group or family can muster some self-awareness, the rebel can function as a signpost for hypocrisy or dishonesty.

In a dysfunctional group, the rebel becomes the focus of attention, allowing the other members to unite in disapproval. In this way, the rebel can be used to deflect attention from group dysfunction and group secrets, even as he is trying to expose those secrets.

The Downside: When rebels grow up, they can attain a level of peace with themselves and society while enjoying the freedom that comes from not being afraid to challenge the status quo. However, Rebels who don't find peace and maturity can make poor decisions and engage in risky behavior. As a result, the Rebel who is stuck in the role can have trouble keeping a job, developing a career, or staying out of trouble with the law. Compulsive rebellion also prevents the Rebel from facing his own problems and taking responsibility for his own life. The Rebel is glamorized in movies, but onscreen rebels often die young.

Scapegoat

Scapegoats get blamed for anything that goes wrong in the system. The Scapegoat is seen as odd, difficult, or different from the norm in personality or appearance, or both. The Scapegoat doesn't fit in. This gives the other group members permission to treat the Scapegoat with contempt or even anger. The function of the Scapegoat in a dysfunctional group system is to allow the group to evade self-scrutiny and responsibility for its dysfunctions. Instead of addressing group problems, the other group members blame the Scapegoat.

The Downside: Other than developing a tough skin, there's not much of an upside to being a Scapegoat. Being scapegoated can leave scars. Scapegoats can suffer a loss of self-esteem and develop an uncertainty about life and relationships. If scapegoated in childhood, the role can become part of their identity, who they think they are—odd, different, to blame, even when they don't know what they're to blame for.

Hero/Star

The Hero does most things right. He shines and excels. Heroes are responsible, ambitious, and nice. They make the family proud and do well in school, either academically or in sports, or both. The Hero exemplifies group values and obeys the group's code of acceptable behavior.

The Hero gives the group something to focus on, to hold up as a model. This can be a good thing, but sometimes the focus on the Hero takes attention and value away from other members of the group. Because the Hero is a model of acceptable behavior, she can make it harder for other members of the group to be "different" or to challenge the system.

The Downside: Everyone has a dark side, and most people need time out of the limelight. The Hero is always "on" and therefore needs to be perfect. This can be like wearing a straitjacket, and if the Hero really buys into the role, it cuts off access to numerous other facets of his personality. The Hero who can't take time out from the role can have difficulty accepting his own flaws. He can also find it hard to come to terms with the fact that stardom often fades with age.

The Problem One

The Problem One in a group is seen as sickly, different, addicted, intellectually challenged, depressed, or afflicted in any other way that allows the group to identify them as having a problem. The Problem One is different from the Rebel, who challenges the group values, and from the Scapegoat, who gets blamed for anything that goes wrong in the system. The Problem One has problems that other group members can rally around and try to fix.

This role is most common in families. Families often take their problem child to therapy, but a good systemic therapist will broaden the focus of therapy to include the entire family. In a family, a problem child can offer parents a way to avoid looking at the problems in their own relationship.

The Downside: Problem Ones need to be taken care of, and this need can carry through into adult relationships. If the Problem One sees himself as perpetually defective in some way, he may cut himself off from the world of vibrant, healthy living.

Fixer/Caretaker/Placater

The Caretaker's life revolves around helping people, "fixing" them, making them better, happier, jollier. The Caretaker tries to calm storms and smooth out relationships, to make everything okay. In moderation, this role can make group/family life smoother, but when done compulsively, it's less about creating a healthy group and more about avoiding conflict. Conflict is essential for the development of intimacy in a group, so avoiding it means the group avoids an essential part of its development.

The Downside: Lots of people get stuck in the Caretaker role, particularly women. It's an aspect of codependent relationships. Being a Caretaker can lead people down a narrow path where they lose sight of themselves in relationships with others. Caretakers suppress their own needs and desires in order to serve others. Because they don't assert themselves and set clear boundaries, Caretakers can end up in abusive relationships or relationships where they're not treated with respect and consideration.

Helpless One

The Helpless role is more often filled by women than by men. Many women begin playing helpless to avoid outshining or challenging a man. In groups, the Helpless One is seen as being less capable than the other members of the group. Other members look out for the Helpless One, help him with his tasks, and generally accept that he won't be able to accomplish much without getting help.

The Helpless role differs from the Problem One because the Helpless One is merely helpless. They're not the central focus of group attention in the way the Problem One often is. The effect of this role is to create good feeling in those who do the "helping," who take on jobs the Helpless One can't handle. In time, this helping out can lead to resentment.

The Downside: Helplessness is disabling. Because he plays this role, the Helpless One may not learn the skills necessary to survive in the world independently. Of course, Helpless Ones often attract people who take care of them, so learning basic living skills is not always necessary for survival. However, if we want to inhabit the full spectrum of who we are, then remaining "helpless" will hold us back. It can also leave us open to feeling controlled in relationships and set adrift when there's nobody around to take care of us.

Leader

Leaders, whether they are given the title of leader or not, inspire, direct, and hold the vision for the group. They have a knack for taking the group in a given direction, whether they are out front in doing so or are subtly empowering and encouraging from behind. The Leader plays an important role in the group, but a Leader's time comes and goes. Problems can arise when the Leader has trouble stepping aside to make way for new leadership to emerge. In this case, the Leader can block the development of the group.

The Downside: Leadership can be a lonely position. If someone over-identifies with leadership, as with any role, they find it hard to step out of it. They're never off duty. Leaders can find it hard to be anonymous, to be ordinary, to get things wrong. They can find it especially hard to be led by others.

WHEN ROLES BECOME A PROBLEM

In some groups, I am a quiet, passive follower of the leader. In others, I'm outspoken and often the one who names the proverbial elephant in the room. I don't really mind which role I play in a group as long as I can move out of that role if I choose to do so. When we have the freedom to explore different roles within our family or other groups, roles can be vehicles to explore the infinite fascinating aspects of ourselves.

A role becomes a problem when we hide behind it or over-identify with it. When this happens, we become locked into our role. Being locked into a role can feel as suffocating and debilitating as being locked into an iron mask. A locked-in role is a formidable barrier to self-exploration and spiritual growth. My client Orla could testify to this.

Thirty-five years after the event, Orla could remember her first day at elementary school in vivid detail. Lunchtime had been the worst part of the day. Five-year-old Orla huddled against the wall of the school, clutching the book bag her mother had given her. A teacher crouched down next to her. Orla could still remember the woman's face close to hers—short salt-and-pepper hair, a sharp nose, concerned eyes.

"Why don't you go and play with the others?" the teacher asked.

Orla clung tighter to her book bag and shook her head, too afraid to move.

For the first few years in school, Orla's shyness crippled her socially. But she was a bright child, full of ideas, and somehow in her quiet way, she got things done. Other children asked her for help with homework and projects, and she always obliged. As the years passed, her classmates sought her opinion not just about homework but on what they should wear and how to manage friendships, problems with brothers and sisters, and problems with parents. They looked to Orla for direction and almost always followed her suggestions.

Orla began to embrace the role of Leader. Her shyness abated, so by the time she got to tenth grade, Orla was the center of a group of friends who, every week, collected food donations, which they distributed to people in their neighborhood who were homeless and in need. Under Orla's direction, the little group of volunteers worked out arrangements with local grocery stores and supermarkets. The store owners donated their day-old bread and unsold vegetables. By the time Orla graduated from college, the volunteer food collection had grown into a food bank and then became a registered nonprofit, with Orla as the director.

The role of Leader "took her out of herself," as Orla's mother described it. In a buoyant economy, Orla led the nonprofit into political lobbying on behalf of people who are poor and homeless. She became "high-profile," gave interviews on radio and TV, and mixed with politicians. Her parents were happy to see their shy daughter blossom into a confident, successful young woman.

A decade later, however, the economy had gone into recession, and the food bank's board of management believed food distribution was more important than political activism. Orla disagreed. She fought openly with board members and refused to lead the change of direction. Her stubbornness surprised everyone, including Orla. As sometimes happens in organizations, the board of management decided that their leader had reached the limits of her vision. Nobody wanted Orla to leave completely, but the chairman of the board asked her to resign as director.

Orla, then in her late thirties, fell into depression punctuated with attacks of anxiety.

Roles can give us the opportunity to explore aspects of our personality that normally remain hidden, even to ourselves. Through playing a variety of roles in different groups and circumstances, we get to experience the full range of who we are. As a result, confidence can emerge from behind shyness, vulnerability from toughness, allure from prudishness. This is what Orla thought had happened to her. She believed the confident, socially adept woman hidden inside her had been drawn into the light through her role as a leader.

SELF-IMAGE

Over four hundred years ago, in his play *As You Like It*, William Shakespeare wrote these famous lines: "All the world's a stage, and all the men and women merely players. They have their exits and their entrances, and one man in his time plays many parts." In healthy groups, we enter and we exit our roles. When we identify with a role, however, that role becomes who we are, our self-image. A self-image is how we present ourselves to the world, and in time we can come to believe the image is who we are. People can identify with their job, for example. They can see themselves as a business person, teacher, or lawyer rather than someone who works in business, education, or the law. Parents can identify with being a mother or father. We can identify with being beautiful, sexy, shy, dependent, competent, successful, or a failure. Even depression can become a self-image.

If we believe the image is who we are, we know no other way to be. We confuse our role with our Big Self, and the depth of identification with the role or image squeezes out awareness. It can be difficult to connect with our Big Self when we are imprisoned in our Small Self identity. We can lose touch with who we are at the core. The role can act as a barrier to that real, direct, authentic interaction with life that oneness with self offers us. And if we are not authentically showing up for life, if we are insulated behind a role, the joy of mystical experience can be cut off to us. Often we become aware of how much we have identified with a self-image only when that image is challenged, as it was for Orla.

Orla reacted badly to changes in the organization she had founded. Panic alternated with rage, all with an underlay of depression. Her behavior mystified her colleagues. Why couldn't she just move with the times? Or move out of the organization? Orla asked herself the same questions during her first therapy session.

THE FIRST PRACTICE: AWARENESS AND ROLES

Orla's iron mask had a velvet lining. Shy, terrified Orla found confidence, social poise, and power in the role of Leader. The process of hiding behind a role is similar to an actor playing a role in a movie or play. The difference between acting and identifying with a role is that an actor knows he's acting. Orla didn't know she was hiding behind her role of Leader/Director. For Orla, she and her role and image had become one. When we identify this closely with a role, the gap between us and the role needs to be pried open. This happens when life shakes us up a little, the way it shook up Orla. Then and only then did the first flickering of awareness emerge in her consciousness.

When I first met Orla, she seemed so forlorn that I asked her to give herself a break, maybe go out with friends for an evening. As often happens in therapy, a simple question can turn the conversation in an unexpected direction. Orla looked as if she had a great social life, but every party or reception she attended related to work. Director Orla sparkled at parties, but when she accepted an invitation to a night out that was not work-related, she felt so uncomfortable that she invariably left early "to catch up on work." Because she was locked into her mask of confidence, she never learned to develop real confidence. For forty-year-old Orla, that journey lay ahead.

Many of the people I've met who are stuck in roles don't know the discontent they feel is role-related. But unlike Orla, they do know something is not right in their life.

People who are aware of their role-related discontent:

- often long to be something other than who they are, to jump out of their own skin and be a different person, if only for a little while.

- can feel condemned to fulfill other people's expectations of who they should be and how they should behave.
- try hard to either meet or compulsively rebel against those expectations.
- feel trapped in the circumstances of their life, stuck in a rut.

If you suspect you might be stuck in a role, here is an exercise in role awareness.

EXERCISE 34: AM I STUCK IN MY ROLE OR IMAGE?

Take a pen and paper and divide the page into two columns. Choose a group you're currently involved with, such as your family. In the column on the left-hand side of the page, describe yourself as you are in that group. Use no more than three words. Here are some examples:

I AM ...
soft, caring, gentle
wild, forceful, strong
incapable, meek, dependent
successful, admired, self-contained
beautiful/handsome, charming, good

In the right-hand column, write three more words, words that to you are the opposite of what you wrote in the first column. Just write. Don't pass judgment on the words you use. These are just descriptions. If you're involved in more than one group, as most of us are, you can repeat the exercise for each group. Use the examples here as a guide.

I AM ...	I COULD BE ...
soft, caring, gentle	strong, decisive, task-focused
wild, forceful, strong	conforming, gentle, sensible
incapable, meek, dependent	competent, independent, assertive
successful, admired, self-contained	vulnerable, retiring, anonymous
beautiful/handsome, charming, good	plain, ordinary, devious

Now review your list. Ask yourself, "If I wanted to, in this group, could I be the person I described in the second column?" If you are caring and gentle, could you also be strong, decisive, and task-oriented? If you are strong and decisive, could you allow yourself to be vulnerable in your chosen group? If you are rebellious, could you also conform? If not, then perhaps you've become stuck in your role, your image.

Whether we suddenly become aware of our mask through life events or we identify that being stuck in a role is at the basis of a growing dissatisfaction with our life, the origins of our difficulty often lie in our past. If we want to discover why we took on that role, if we want to break its grip on us, we often need to look backward. Looking back can herald a journey into darkness, and this is where the third and fourth practices are useful.

THE THIRD AND FOURTH PRACTICES:
TRUST AND OPENNESS, GROWING FROM ADVERSITY

If we look back to our family of origin, we may begin to unravel the mystery of why we donned our own mask in the first place. Orla is a good example. Orla claimed to have come from a "happy" family where "everyone loved each other." She described both her parents as successful, which meant they had high-profile jobs within their fields. As therapy progressed, Orla's Inner Witness revealed the dark side of her parents' ambition.

Orla's parents demanded that their child also be successful. They chose criticism as their method of fostering drive and ambition in their daughter. Orla's mother criticized the way Orla tied her shoe-laces, the few extra pounds she carried around her belly, and the Bs Orla occasionally got in school instead of As. Criticism drove Orla to excel in school, but it also magnified her natural shyness. When the role of Leader emerged throughout her late childhood, Orla latched on to it, much to her parents' relief. Leadership seemed to solve all of Orla's problems and at the same time satisfy her parents.

The lessons we learn about ourselves as children can drive us toward a role. The particular lessons are unique to each individual. In Orla's case, a belief that she was a failure drove her to succeed. As a result, the real, painfully shy Orla disappeared from view along with her ability to live a full, free life. Given a different set of circumstances, the belief that she was a failure could have driven Orla into the role of Helpless One, Problem One, or even Rebel.

Awareness drives a wedge between us and our role and cracks open a vital space for us to grow. For some people, this is immediately liberating. Others, like Orla, flounder around in a void of confusion, not knowing who they are or what to do with themselves. Awareness can take us behind our role, behind our self-image. What we find there can be painful. It's not always easy to explore our past.

It's not always easy to face the beliefs we have about ourselves that drive us to hide behind a role.

This is the time to trust the darkness. The foundering period is a chrysalis from which a more authentic identity and purpose in life can emerge. With time, trust, and support, the contours of our Big Self emerge from the darkness.

EXERCISE 35: WHERE MY ROLES COME FROM

Re-read the list of roles earlier in this chapter. Then practice the anchoring meditation (exercise 5) from chapter 4. When you have established your breathing pattern, visualize a place where you feel both safe and free. This is your cocoon. Look around your cocoon, smell the fragrances, feel the textures, get cozy. As you settle into your special place, a TV screen appears before you and it's running a TV show about your life. The episode running right now is you in elementary school. Watch your past unfold before you. What are you doing? Are you interacting with the other children? You go from group to group, in the playground, in the classroom, in the gym. Is there a pattern in the way you interact with your classmates, with your teachers? Do you play a role, perhaps more than one role? When you feel ready, gently take leave of the characters in the movie, and your special place, and return to the present. Are any of the roles you played reflected in your present life?

Elementary school is an important place in the life of a child and can be an incubator of future roles. But family can be even more influential. Revisiting the family of origin can also be traumatic for some people. If you are comfortable with revisiting your family of origin, let's watch a second movie. Go to your safe place as previously instructed. When you feel ready, run the TV show of your life again, but this episode is the one where you interact with your family of origin. See if there's a connection between the role you played in your family and the dominant role in your life right now. The roles you play are not you. Live with that thought for a few days. If it leads you to question who you are without your role, pay particular attention to the next section of this chapter and the exercises that follow it.

The Fifth Practice: Oneness

The board of management wrenched Orla's role from her, but the opposite is more often the case. As soon as we begin to kick against our role, a dysfunctional group kicks back. At one point in my life, I began to speak up for myself instead of going along with what other people wanted. A member of a group I was in at the time took me aside and told me that my behavior "didn't suit me." In truth, it didn't suit her, but I certainly felt the pressure to stay in my role.

Group members have expectations of each other. The Helpless One is expected to need help, the Joker to entertain, the Problem One to be a problem. This pressure to conform is not necessarily malicious or even conscious. But if the Helpless One begins doing things for himself, if the Joker shows anger or sadness, if the Problem One begins to succeed, the system can be thrown into disarray.

At times like this, we can retreat into our old role, like a tortoise retreating into his shell at the first sign of danger. In an extremely dysfunctional group, our attempts to shed a role can unleash a torrent of anger and criticism. Even in groups that are basically loving, one member's efforts to move out of their traditional role can provoke discomfort and criticism. Moving out of the role is a process of negotiation with friends and family, a series of small steps as we, and they, adjust to the change in the group dynamic.

But often the majority of the criticism we dread comes from ourselves. Let's go back to Orla. Behind Orla's mask, she was, in her own words, a shy, socially incompetent failure. "Shy" and "incompetent" were words Orla used like lashes, whipping herself daily. Orla was shy. She was socially incompetent. These are descriptions of fact, a realistic starting point to work from. But by making them into condemnations of herself, Orla reinforced all the criticism she had endured from her mother.

We are pushed toward and drawn into roles because of our life experience and conditioning. Orla was drawn to leadership because she believed herself to be a failure. A Caretaker may be drawn to caring for others because he feels unlovable unless he lavishes love on others. The specifics of why we play out a role are unique to each individual, so the path out of that role is also unique to each person. There is no one map or formula that fits every requirement. But no matter what method we use to free ourselves from our iron mask, it will be made more difficult by self-criticism.

The first practice, Radical Awareness, lifts the cover off our well of self-criticism, and we must deal with what emerges. The most effective antidote to self-criticism is compassion. Compassion for ourselves comes from the mystical experience of oneness with our Big Self. Orla's breakthrough came in a breathwork session when she finally found compassion for her shy, socially incompetent self—the real Orla behind her mask, not Orla as she should be, might be, would be.

Somewhere beneath our imprisonment in a role lies the belief that without that role, we'd be less than adequate, less than acceptable. Moments of unconditional love free us from that belief, and therein lies freedom from being stuck in a role. There may be lots more work to do—we may need to manage our lapses into self-criticism, to explore our past, to negotiate change with our group. But through all of this work, the love we experience through moments of oneness supports and invites us to discard our personal iron mask.

EXERCISE 36: BREAK THE MASK:
ELIMINATE SELF-CRITICISM (A TWO-DAY EXERCISE)

Day 1: Take a notebook and pen with you everywhere you go, and write down all the things you criticize yourself for. Self-criticism can be second nature to us, so you may need to be particularly vigilant to catch yourself in the act. When you have a list of the things you criticize yourself for, find a place where you can be alone and uninterrupted. Once again, practice the anchoring meditation (exercise 5) from chapter 4, and this time, when the rhythm of your breath has been established, visualize a child before you. Notice the child's hair, eyes, the expression on their face, what they're wearing. Then slowly and deliberately begin to criticize that child using items from the list you created throughout the day. Can you get through the list? Can you tell a child all the things you tell yourself? If you can't criticize a child, is it okay to criticize yourself in this way?

Day 2: Once again work with your notepad and pen. This time, when you write down something critical about yourself, tear that strip off the page and throw it into the trash or recycling bin. You will need to do this consciously, with full awareness. Once it's in the bin, direct your mind elsewhere, to your work, your breathing, to whatever you're doing at the time. That particular criticism may arise again later. If it does, repeat the process. Like meditation, this is a discipline that requires practice. But the more you eliminate self-criticism, the closer you come to oneness with yourself and life.

12

VALUES:

Finding Our Own Simplest Truths

Respect the chemistry.

~WALTER WHITE, *BREAKING BAD*

Walter White knows how to make bodies disappear: dissolve them in acid. The antihero of the TV show *Breaking Bad*, Walt cooks the purest, cleanest crystal meth ever to hit the streets of Albuquerque, New Mexico. Hunted by both the police and the drug cartels, Walt scrambles his way through the underworld of illegal drugs. Along the way he lies, he steals, and, when required, he commits the odd murder.

By day, Walter White is a model of middle-class values. He's everything he's supposed to be: a dedicated, hard-working high school teacher, a family man, and a home owner with two cars and a second child on the way. Walt has a problem, though. He has lung cancer, and his teacher's health insurance won't pay for the treatment he needs. So what's a brilliant chemistry teacher to do? Manufacture a top-of-the-range product and go into business.

As a middle-class family man, Walt is expected to obey certain codes of behavior: show appropriate gratitude when his cancer goes into remission, find just the right words of inspiration for the high school student body, play sociable at pool parties, etc. But Walt can't do it. He can't say the right thing at the right time. Because he struggles to follow convention, Walt's behavior grows increasingly bizarre in the eyes of his colleagues and family.

What family and friends don't see is that Walt's descent into the underworld has stripped him of almost every value he ever held dear. To Walt, playing nice after experiencing the life-and-death rawness of the street is meaningless. After everything he was brought up to believe in has been taken away, Walt's remaining values are to provide for his family and respect his craft, respect the chemistry.

Our value system can serve us well, but it can also insulate us from fully experiencing life, from getting to know who we really are. Our value system can also prevent us from letting go into the mystical experience of oneness. Because *Breaking Bad* systematically dismantles Walt's entire value system before our eyes, the show invites us to explore our own values. It invites us to pare away what we've been told is important so we can uncover what's really important to us, what author Charles Dickens called our "simplest truths."

IDENTIFYING VALUES

A value is something we consider to be good, right, fair, appropriate. Values can be categorized under headings such as social, political, religious, personal, moral, cultural, and more. We value things like success, material comfort, drive, ambition, and, in some situations, ruthlessness and cunning. We also value kindness, stability, integrity, bravery, patriotism, honesty, love, and spiritual awareness. The list of values is long. Like roles, values can enhance our engagement with life. Values can also function as the walls of an open-air prison, cutting us off from our spiritual nature. For this reason, it's important to get to know our own values.

The first step in exploring this topic is to identify our own values. One of the simplest ways to do this is with another starter-sentence exercise.

EXERCISE 37: EXPLORING VALUES

Take a notepad and pen and divide the page into two columns. In the left-hand column, complete the sentence "I should ..." over and over until there are no more "shoulds." The words "I should ..." could be replaced with "It's right that I ..." or "It's appropriate that I ..." with the same effect. Here's an example:

I SHOULD ...
I should be nice to people.
I should be generous.
I should have a new car.
I should have my own business.
I should be married.
I should support the troops.
I should always pay my taxes.
I should have a nicer house and a pool.

Review your list carefully, then in the next column write down the values you think might underpin your "shoulds." Here's an example for the previous list:

I should …	Possible Value/s
I should be nice to people.	*Conformity, niceness, politeness*
I should be generous.	*Generosity*
I should have a new car.	*Money, image*
I should have my own business.	*Ambition, success*
I should be married.	*Coupling, marriage, having a partner*
I should support the troops.	*Patriotism*
I should always pay my taxes.	*Honesty, obeying the rules, conformity*
I should have a nicer house and a pool.	*Materialism, comfort, luxury*

Now that we have become aware of our existing values, the next step in the exercise is to observe our reaction to those values. Do we approve of our values and praise ourselves for having such a right and appropriate belief system? Do we reject any of our values, distance ourselves from them slightly, or criticize ourselves for holding such a belief? Do we defend the value: "What's wrong with wanting a nice home?" "What's wrong with wanting to protect my country?"

All of these reactions are signals that direct us to dig deeper. If we are completely comfortable with our values, then when we identify those values, our reaction will be minimal. For example, if I have brown hair and I'm happy with the color, then when someone points out that I have brown hair, I will have no reaction. However, if I am consciously or unconsciously critical of my hair color, I may defend it or apologize for it, or I might recite the virtues of brown hair. If we have a strong reaction to one of our values—approval, disapproval, or defense—that value may be built on shaky ground. It may not be one of our simplest truths. It may be a barrier to deep connection with our Big Self, a barrier to oneness.

When we've identified our values and observed our reaction to those values, we can proceed to the next step of this awareness exercise. We can search for the origins of our beliefs. Why do we believe what we believe? Where do our cherished values really come from?

WHERE VALUES COME FROM

I recently attended a workshop on root cause analysis—how to find the root cause of a problem. One of the methods offered by the instructor was the Five Whys, a famous problem-solving technique developed by Sakichi Toyoda, the founder of Toyota Industries. For every problem, ask "why?" at least five times. The Five Whys method is intended for use in business, but it's an equally effective method for uncovering the origin of values. So when some colleagues agreed with each other about how important it is to set goals in life, I asked them why. Here's how the sequence went:

1. Why set goals?
   "So you can accomplish things."
2. Why accomplish things?
   "So you can make something of yourself."
3. Why do you want to make something of yourself?
   "So you can improve."
4. Why do you want to improve yourself?
   "Because you're supposed to improve yourself."
5. Why are you supposed to improve yourself?
   "Everybody wants to improve. That's the way it is."

I've moved in many different social groups. For some of those groups, the idea of setting goals is meaningless. For others, that drive to achieve, to constantly improve, is a moral touchstone. In the estimation of groups that value goal setting, people without the ambition to improve themselves can be suspect or even flawed. The group's behavioral norm is to strive, achieve, and improve. This is the opposite of the mystical state of oneness, where all striving falls away and we rest in total acceptance of the present moment. The answer my colleagues gave to the fifth why is revealing. We should set goals in life because everybody does. In other words, that's what society has told us to do.

The purpose of questioning the practice of goal setting is not to imply that goal setting is bad or wrong in any way. The exercise is about revealing the origin of the values that underpin our behavior. It took my colleagues just five whys to trace one of their most cherished values—self-improvement—back to the society in which they grew up. We're told what's important by our parents, our community, our church, the media. But if nobody told us what is important, what would we choose to make important in life? What is our version of respecting the chemistry? What is our simplest truth?

Let's look more closely at a few of the values from the list in exercise 37.

NICENESS

One of my most memorable mystical experiences happened while I was being mugged. I had parked my car near my in-laws' house in a less than savory neighborhood in Dublin. After spending an enjoyable evening downtown with friends, one friend and I returned to the car for the drive home. The attack happened just as we reached the car, and the target was the purse strapped across my shoulder. Three men swooped down on us. Suddenly hands were everywhere. I hunched over the purse and screamed. My friend threw punches over my head. Then someone hit me on the chin. My face turned skyward, and I found myself staring into a vast indigo dome studded with stars. I remember thinking how beautiful it was, examining the stars and being aware that there was no moon. Then I heard my own voice, and it was magnificent. Through my voice I expanded into the sky, filling it, becoming the space between the sky and the ground. I was having a wonderful time. But I was also under attack, and my cosmic adventure wasn't really helping with the practicalities. I needed to do something, so I lashed out blindly with my feet, kicking anything I could touch. Then, as suddenly as it had begun, the attack ended, probably because a light came on in a house near us. The three men dissolved into the night, leaving me with my purse.

The mugging could have been traumatic, but it wasn't. Thanks to the mystical state I flipped into during the attack, the experience turned out well for me. But it didn't have to happen at all. I could have avoided the attack. I got mugged that night for one reason only: one of my most ingrained values overrode both my gut instinct and my common sense.

I was brought up to value being nice to people. At all costs, be polite, be nice. I have an intense dislike of tea, but I grew up in a country where tea was the standard drink, offered to all guests as a sign of welcome. The host likely did not have another beverage on hand, so if a guest refused tea, it could throw the host into confusion. I've lost count of the number of times I forced myself, gagging and heaving, to knock back cups of tea, all to avoid any possible inconvenience to my host. The "niceness" value was so much a part of my existence that I knew no other way to be. That value kicked in again on the night I was mugged.

Before the attack, from the opposite side of the street, my friend and I could see the glitter of shattered glass on the ground around my car. The rear window had been smashed. The moment I saw the glass, I registered the other signs of danger: men standing at strategic points on the street, low whistles that carried secret signals. Then, as I neared the back of the car, a man approached us. He sympathized with me about the window and offered to get me a replacement for less than I'd pay in a repair shop. He looked directly into my face and held out his hand so we could shake on the deal.

I knew what the man was. I knew what he was about to do. And I knew what I needed to do. I needed to speak to him in his language, to tell him to fuck off, and to do it at the top of my voice. Given the location of the car, close to houses and a busy intersection, yelling would have shown him that mugging us would not be worth the risk. But I couldn't shake off the value that said "be nice to people." Instead of yelling at the man, I politely shook his hand and thanked him for his concern. Seconds later, his friends emerged from the shadows, and the mugging I had anticipated began.

Being nice to each other makes the world an easier, gentler place to be. Over the years, I've heard many people praise niceness as a virtue. There is nothing inherently wrong with being nice, when nice is appropriate. It was not appropriate that night in Dublin. That night, one of my most ingrained, positive values separated me from my own intuition, and in the process helped get me mugged. There are many other, less dramatic situations in which being nice is neither appropriate nor beneficial. Niceness can lead us to:

- say yes, when we mean no.
- go along with something we fundamentally disagree with.
- stand by while injustices are perpetrated.
- refrain from having tough conversations.
- accept poor treatment.

Every item on this list, over time, can have serious consequences. Let's take the example of tough conversations. In every relationship—intimate, parental, friendship, or at work—conflicts arise. It can be difficult for two people to start a conversation about a problem. All sorts of fears about losing the relationship can kick in, but often our reluctance is due to the fact that we've been brought up to believe we shouldn't disconcert others. We should be nice. If we're too nice to tackle a problem with a work colleague who never meets deadlines, for example, chances are that colleague will continue to miss deadlines. We may be evolved enough to put up with delayed and bungled projects. More likely, however, we will build up a store of resentment toward our colleague. That resentment can come out in indirect and not so nice ways.

Relationship problems don't go away because we're too nice to tackle them. The problem usually gets worse over time. The relationship and the people involved in it suffer as a result. In these situations, the belief that we should always be nice to each other can do far more harm than expressing genuine anger or frustration upfront.

PATRIOTISM

A few years ago, on an almost empty flight, an Iraq and Afghan War veteran asked if he could sit beside me. He couldn't sleep. Neither could I. So we spent the best part of two hours talking. We didn't exchange names, so I'll call him Don. Like many other young men and women, he enlisted after 9/11. He had just completed his third tour in a war zone and expected to be discharged shortly. That night he was heading home for Thanksgiving.

Don didn't talk about combat. But on that hushed night flight, he did talk about 9/11. He described his feelings right after the attack on the World Trade Center—the love he felt for his country, the pride he felt in the flag his father raised on their front lawn, and the anger he felt toward the terrorists who attacked his homeland. Patriotism drove him to enlist in the army. His parents blessed his decision.

Don anticipated the scene waiting for him when our plane landed, his mother crying, his father's big bear hug. They would kiss him, fuss over him, and feed him whether he was hungry or not. Don's family believed in the conventional trajectory of life—graduate from college, get a job, marry, buy a house, have children, go to church. At the big family Thanksgiving celebration, aunts, uncles, and cousins would welcome him home and thank him for his service to his country.

In 2001, Don shared his family's values. Back then, he envisioned a future with a steady job, a home, and children of his own. Like his family, he also believed in freedom, democracy, and love of country, and that the war would protect those values. Everything changed when he was shipped overseas.

For Don, the men in his troop in Iraq had become both his country and his family. Now, just a few Thanksgivings later, his loyalty lay with his fellow soldiers, not his homeland or politicians or a cause. And that night, the thing he dreaded most was the hero's welcome that friends and family had planned for him on Thanksgiving Day. Don's chosen buffer against that dread was alcohol. By the time we reached our destination, he was well on his way to being drunk.

It's an old story of war. When life is stripped down to a matter of living or dying, all those values we think are so important lose their significance. Like Walter White, my young veteran companion had been stripped of the values that once gave meaning to his life, stripped of them in the most traumatic way possible.

When life takes away our values in the way it did for Don and the fictional Walter White, we can be left foundering. We find ourselves out of sync with the people we've known all our life, out of step with that life. Most of us don't have to face our values in such a traumatic way, but if we want to engage fully with life, if we want to be our most authentic self, we are well advised to scrutinize our own values.

Now that we understand the role values play in our lives, let's complete our exercise in awareness by going to the source of our value system.

EXERCISE 38: WHERE MY VALUES COME FROM

Choose one of the values you identified in your list from exercise 37. Practice the Five Whys technique outlined earlier in this chapter. Write down your answer to each "why?" When you get to the root of your value, ask yourself, "Is this value one of my simplest truths?"

THE FIFTH PRACTICE: ONENESS AND VALUES

Values can be deceptive. What at first glance appears life-enhancing can actually be a major obstacle on the road to spiritual fulfillment. What is appropriate in one situation might be detrimental in another. And the values that are important to us in one stage of life can lose their meaning as we mature.

Unexamined values can have consequences. Don's unquestioned patriotism got him into a war he later regretted, a war that left him adrift in a life without meaning. On a less serious level, my niceness got me mugged. But the limiting effect of unquestioned values is usually more subtle.

During my college years, I volunteered with an organization called the Simon Community. The Simon, as it was called, distributed soup and sandwiches nightly to people in Dublin who were homeless. Through volunteering, I got to know many of the men and women who slept rough on the city streets. One morning, as I waited at a downtown bus stop, a man with the cut-up face of a homeless alcoholic worked the bus line. He didn't speak but held out his hand to each person in the line, silently begging for change. I knew him from my Friday night soup run and said hello. But when he turned to the woman standing just ahead of me in the line, she pointedly turned her back to him.

I've encountered that attitude toward people who are poor countless times since then. The attitude stems from the kind of values Don once espoused without question. We often value a lifestyle that involves a job, hard work, home ownership, good schools for the children, and involvement in a church. There's absolutely nothing wrong with any of this—unless we get so involved in our lifestyle values that we become cut off from any other way of being.

The step from entrenched, unquestioned values to prejudice is a short one. It's easy to look at people who are different, who do not share our values, as inferior, wrong, or less than equal. Pema Chödrön writes, "When we make things wrong, we do it out of a desire to obtain some kind of ground or security."[37] This points to a need for awareness on a deeper, more radical level. If we explore the roots of our values, we can uncover our insecurities. When we cling tightly to a value and make its opposite wrong or "less than" in some way, it's often because we ourselves need something to feel good and right about. In the process, we create duality, the opposite of oneness, and our lives are diminished as a result.

Our lives are diminished because entrenched values cut us off from potential experiences. Experience stretches us, pulls us out of our comfort zone and into liminal space, the place beyond what's comfortable. Liminal space is not an easy place to be, but it is where we grow and where we often encounter our Big Self. Liminal space can lead directly to the mystical experience of oneness. The man at the bus stop is long since dead. I didn't find being with him easy, but I still remember him vividly. I remember what he awakened in me every time I met him: compassion. For the few minutes it took me to hand him soup and a sandwich, he did me the favor of connecting me with my own spiritual nature. My life would have been a little bit less rich had I not known him.

Mystical experience shows us the incalculable value of oneness. Oneness is a state of pure love, love that is not earned by towing the line, conforming to a code of behavior, or espousing particular values. In a state of oneness, we simply exist, we are. This is often referred to as "I am-ness." I am! Not "I am a man, a woman, a parent, friend, teacher, janitor, CEO ..." Not "I am good, bad, patriotic, helpful, angry, successful ..." Simply "I am." Period. End to thinking about it. That deep connection with life informs our behavior, but if we act out of our Big Selves, we do not need to identify with any particular value system, or to hide behind one. We no longer need to make others wrong or less than.

Many paths lead to the experience of oneness. One of those paths is communion with other people, particularly people who can challenge us spiritually. Entrenched values, unquestioned values, can divert us from that path, can cut us off from the opportunity to experience our own authentic Big Self, through oneness with others.

EXERCISE 39: BEYOND VALUES, ONENESS

Seat yourself comfortably in a place where you won't be interrupted. Use the twenty connected breaths (exercise 12) from chapter 6. Breathe comfortably and rhythmically until your breathing pattern has been established. Nestle yourself into your special place, your cocoon, and get comfortable there. Then begin to visualize the values you identified in your list from exercise 37 earlier in this chapter. Give them a color, a symbol, or whatever image comes to mind to represent each value. Take each value and place it to one side, just out of your field of vision. Then, with every inhale, breathe in the sentence "I am who I am." When this feels comfortable to you, shorten it to "I am." Notice how that feels in your body. When you feel ready, complete your visualization by gently returning to the room where you are seated.

13
FINDING TRUE LOVE

There is nothing so clear-sighted as true love, nothing.
~ANTHONY DE MELLO

One of the most influential books about romantic love was written by a Frenchman, Andreas Capellanus. In his book *De Amore (On Love: A Treatise on Courtly Love)*, Capellanus attempted to describe romantic love in terms of rules. Here is an edited version of Capellanus's rules:

- When a lover suddenly has sight of his beloved, his heart beats wildly.
- He who is vexed by the thoughts of love eats little and seldom sleeps.
- A lover can never have enough of the embraces of his beloved.

- The true lover is continuously obsessed with the image of his beloved.

- True jealousy always increases the effects of love.

- If a lover suspects another, jealousy and the effects of love increase.

- The slightest suspicion incites the lover to suspect the worse of his beloved.

- The true lover believes only that which he thinks will please his beloved.[38]

The language is a little antiquated, but if these "rules" sound familiar, it's because they are. The rules of love can be found in almost every romance novel, from the relatively chaste Harlequins to bawdy bodice rippers. They can also be found in the many books on modern dating and how to snare and keep a man or woman. Yet these rules are far from modern. Capellanus wrote *De Amore* somewhere between 1184 and 1186.

In the decades before Capellanus penned his possibly satirical analysis of "courtly love,"[39] Eleanor of Aquitaine and her daughter Marie, Countess of Champagne, presided over the French court of Eleanor's husband, King Louis VII. Louis maintained a large court. While the male courtiers took care of business, the women entertained themselves with art, music, and literature. But the ladies of the court grew weary of endless stories about knights and their heroic battles. They wanted stories about women and about the kind of fantasies that appealed to women. So Eleanor filled her court with the roaming troubadour poets of the region. Troubadour poets wrote romantic poetry modeled on the relationship that existed between a knight and his lord. Under Eleanor's patronage, the poets and the ladies of the court refined the concept, rules, and conventions of what became known as courtly love.

Most people have never heard of Capellanus or Eleanor of Aquitaine or the troubadour poets of southern France, but they have shaped our whole concept of love. Their ideas have echoed down through the centuries into music and literature, advertising and film. They're firmly enshrined in our culture and have molded our notion of relationships. The list of rules from *De Amore* is much longer than what I've copied here, but even if we examine just this short sampling, we will find most of the elements of modern romance:

All-Consuming Love: When we fall in love, it is all-consuming. Friends and family recede into the background as our new relationship takes over large parts of our life. We can't stop thinking about the person we're attracted to. We daydream about them and imagine a future together. We can never get enough of them. That's how we "know" it's love. We call it "spark" and "chemistry" and we use it as a guide to whom to pursue a relationship with and whom to bypass or simply be friends with.

Self Given Away: According to Capellanus, true lovers mold themselves to the requirements of their lover. This has been true more for women than men, but both genders have the capacity to reshape themselves to suit their lover. One man I know who hates exercise now rises at 4:00 a.m. to work out with his new girlfriend. Somehow I don't see the early-morning workouts lasting, but some of the adaptations we make for a relationship can be good for us. As Capellanus writes, "love makes an ugly and rude person shine with all beauty, knows how to endow with nobility even one of humble birth." In modern English, we would say that love brings out the best in us and helps us tap into aspects of ourselves that we would not otherwise know existed.

Love can indeed open up new worlds for us to explore, and some of the changes we make for love don't just last, they enhance our lives and nurture our spiritual development. But those adaptations can also shut us down to life and cut us off from our deepest, truest self. I've known many women, for example, who "play stupid" to please their man, or who fade into the background in public so their man can shine.

Jealousy: In the courtly love tradition, love is a game in which men and women tantalize each other, push each other away, and feign a lack of interest to make each other jealous. For some, jealousy is part of the dance of attraction and adds spice to a fledgling relationship. Jealousy is often regarded as a measure of the strength of sexual love. The possessiveness and anger excited by jealousy are often seen as a sign of interest, of being "hooked." The jealous person is hooked, but they're hooked by their own neediness, not by love.

Two Love Stories

Falling in love is truly a wonderful, heady, walking-on-air experience. We feel more alive than we've ever felt before. All is well, we think, and all will be well into the future. In many respects, this mirrors the mystical experience of oneness. It's as if we've become better, fuller versions of ourselves, or, as Capellanus said in *De Amore*, "Oh what a marvellous thing is love, which makes a man shine with so many virtues and which teaches everyone to abound in good customs."

But that falling-in-love feeling doesn't last. When it subsides, our underlying relationship is revealed. That relationship can be life-enhancing and mutually fulfilling. For many couples, relationships are a nurturing, empowering source of joy and contentment. But relationships can also be one of the greatest sources of pain we will ever know, and even relationships we consider reasonably good can hold us back from fully embracing life.

For those who feel diminished by or discontented with their romantic relationships, let's look at a couple of relationships where one or both of the people involved have been held back or damaged by the experience and how they used the five practices to transform both themselves and their relationship.

Mike and Dave: All-Consuming Love

Mike and Dave met when they worked together at an investment bank. Mike was an administrator, and Dave, an accountant. The attraction was instant; "electric" was how Dave described it. Within days they were dating, and after three months they moved in together. Dave recalled how they spent weekends together, seeing no one else, wanting only to bathe in each other's presence. They didn't answer the phone and found meeting friends an intrusion on their precious "special" time together. There was a strong sense of specialness, of "the two of us against the world."

Passion subsided slowly, leaving behind a relationship based on a shared sense of humor and a deep caring for each other. Dave and Mike had bonded and, without really discussing it, began to create a future together. It would take another ten years for Dave to realize his life had shrunk almost to the point of extinction.

Mike suffered from severe anxiety. He disguised it well behind a sharp, intelligent wit, one of the things that so attracted Dave. As they got to know each other, Mike opened up to Dave about his inner turmoil. The two men talked for hours at a stretch about Mike's fears and anxieties.

"It bonded us," Dave explained in a therapy session. "It was like he trusted me and only me."

Mike's anxiety intensified over the years. He cut back to part-time work, while Dave's hours increased to support both of them. Mike began to turn down invitations to parties and dinners and eventually stopped going on vacations with Dave, who loved to travel. Their worlds shrank until Dave, a social extrovert, began to experience prolonged bouts of depression. One of Dave's few remaining friends insisted he find a therapist. In his final therapy session, Dave reviewed his relationship with Mike.

"I used to try to figure the relationship out," he explained. "I loved Mike. I still do, but it was killing me. I gave up everything—my friends, my life—and I didn't even see it happening. We'd end up watching TV every night, just the two of us. We'd have dinner at the same time, watch the same shows, go to bed at the same time, get up at the same time. It was great in the beginning. That's the funny thing. What was great in the beginning wasn't so good in the end."

Mike and Dave had a classically codependent relationship. Codependence is a concept that grew out of Alcoholics Anonymous (AA). AA is one of the most effective systems ever developed for managing addiction, but it didn't take long for the organization's leadership to notice that when an alcoholic stopped drinking, their spouse often ran into trouble. Life with an active alcoholic revolves around alcoholism—containing it, covering for it, managing it. When the drinking stops, the alcoholic's spouse can find themselves adrift without a center in their life. The alcoholic is dependent on alcohol. The spouse is codependent on alcoholism.

The seeds of codependence are sown long before we get into a relationship. Dave, a successful accountant, rising star in his company, and world traveler, had his own well-hidden inadequacies. For most of his life, he had felt worthless and unlovable. He covered it extremely well, and even managed to hide it from himself most of the time. The source of his feelings was his father, who rarely showed affection and criticized and often beat his son. When Dave met Mike, all this changed. Dave felt loved, but more than that, he felt lovable, and taking care of Mike made him feel valuable.

When we're in love, we feel lovable. We feel attractive, desirable, needed, and wanted. We feel an incredible sense of aliveness, a kind of peak state. The hidden danger in such euphoria is that this wonderful ecstatic state depends very much on another human being. That means that for those of us with a fragile Small Self, falling in love is a potential opening into codependence. If someone else makes us feel this alive, this complete, what happens if that other person starts to pull away? And how much will we bend and shape and even jettison ourselves to prevent that pulling away from happening?

In most relationships, the balance of power shifts back and forth between the partners, like taking the lead in a dance—first one person, then the other. In the dance between Dave and Mike, Mike held on to the lead and, from time to time, threatened to leave. The prospect of being left alone terrified Dave, so he trimmed himself and his life to hold on to his partner.

Looking at it from the outside, Dave was the one held back by the relationship. The view from inside the relationship was different. Mike and Dave held each other back in a mutually disabling dance, the steps of which they worked out without knowing what they were doing. Because Mike had the safe cocoon of his relationship, he never had to manage his own anxieties. He never fully inhabited his life. Their dance cut Dave (and Mike) off from his Inner Witness, from awareness, and formed a wall between him and the precious experience of oneness.

Andrew and Linda: Self Given Away

Andrew and Linda met as newly hired graduates at a well-known law firm. Twenty years later, Andrew headed the top-earning mergers and acquisitions department of the company. Linda, who took time off to raise children, was one of two lawyers who handled company wind-downs the law firm offered as a service to existing major clients. Linda was good at her job. In a depressed economy, she could see a lucrative market in company closures and wanted her department to go after the larger company liquidation contracts that had nothing to do with existing clients. She drew up plans for expansion, for reeling in big accounts. But Linda's plans remained just that: plans. She came to therapy frustrated with her lack of ambition and drive.

Linda and Andrew had a solid marriage. They loved each other dearly, with none of the emotional intensity that isolated Dave and

Mike. Andrew and Linda's relationship encompassed family, friends, colleagues, and a healthy social life. It nurtured both partners, which was why Linda's realization came as such a shock to her. During a breathwork session, Linda recognized the unspoken agreement that existed between her and Andrew—he would always be the star performer.

This barely conscious agreement dated back to their earliest years together and spun out through their lives in subtle ways. Linda was a great talker. She could make anything sound bigger and brighter than it actually was. She used most of this talent praising her husband's achievements, not her own, talking up his plans, not her own. When her husband needed help with a case, Linda dropped her own work to assist him. When networking events clashed, the couple always attended the party or dinner that served Andrew's needs, not Linda's.

Andrew never asked Linda to hide her own dreams and showcase his plans instead. He never asked her to mold her life to the requirements of his career or sacrifice her own advancement for his. He didn't have to. At work, at parties, or whenever Linda looked as if she might outshine her husband, subtle signals passed between the couple—so subtle that Linda never consciously registered them. The wordless language that develops between two people who know each other well—such as a faint look of withdrawal on Andrew's face or a petulant set to his lips—told her to back off. Linda learned to be the cheerleader to her stellar husband.

Shocking as the revelation was for Linda, it marked a turning point in her therapy. Her Inner Witness had come to life, and her next job was to answer the question: Why had she taken on the role of cheerleader in the first place?

LOVE AND THE CONTEMPLATIVE MIND

When Linda acknowledged her "contract" and when Dave left Mike, they opened for themselves a way forward. By facing the reality of their situation, they empowered themselves to do something about it, to put the practices to work in their lives.

When Anthony de Mello says, "You say 'I'm in love.' You're not in love, you silly ass. Anytime you're in love … you're being particularly asinine,"[40] he's referring to the fact that falling in love can blind us. It can distract us while another relationship is developing behind the scenes. We discover this hidden relationship when the euphoria of "falling in love" fades. Paradoxically, when we get beyond the "in love" stage, a relationship can become the greatest teacher we will ever have. If we're willing to look, a relationship can reflect back to us aspects of ourselves we didn't know existed or haven't been able to acknowledge. Often, if the relationship is troubled, what it reflects back to us is our own need. Dave needed to be valued. Linda, it turned out, desperately needed to be married.

Can we say we love someone if what we see when we look at them is the fulfillment of our own needs? When we seek happiness exclusively in another person, we can run the risk of seeing in them only what we want to see. We can become blind to the reality of who they really are. Anthony de Mello writes: "When I meet this person, I fall head over heels in love. But have I seen her? No! I'll see her after I marry her, that's when the awakening comes. And that's when love may begin."[41]

Small Self needs often dictate the type of person we're attracted to and drive some of us to choose that same type over and over again with the same results. Ayn Rand elaborates: "Show me the woman he sleeps with and I will tell you his valuation of himself … He will always be attracted to the person who reflects his deepest vision of himself, the woman whose surrender permits him to experience—or to fake—a sense of self-esteem."[42] We can make poor choices when our eyes are blinded by need, and we can develop patterns of relating that may not serve us or our partners well. A solution lies in the first practice.

Radical Awareness: One of my mother's favorite catchphrases was "Love is blind, marriage is an eye-opener." According to Anthony de Mello, real love begins when our eyes open, when we become radically aware. Through awareness, we can begin to explore the role our own Small Self needs to play in our drive to find a partner and in the dynamic we co-create with that partner. Through awareness, we see our own needs, our cravings, and our attachments for what they are—the drivers that propel us to search for happiness outside of ourselves. When our Inner Witness is present to the reality of who we are, then we can be present to the reality of who our lover is, because "there is nothing so clear-sighted as true love, nothing. It's the most clear-sighted thing in the world."[43] Then we can begin to make our already good relationship even better, to resolve the problems in a troubled relationship, or to find happiness alone or with someone new.

Here is an exercise to help us uncover the needs that might lurk beneath the exhilaration of falling in love.

EXERCISE 40: MY RELATIONSHIP NEEDS

If you're in a relationship that's not working or one that has some persistent difficulties, instead of focusing on the other person or the dynamic between you, let's explore the needs you may be trying to meet through your relationship.

First, use whatever breathing exercise from chapter 6 works best for you. When you feel present in your body, make a list of all the things you need from a relationship. Here are some examples: security, to not be alone, to feel normal, to feel whole, financial support, etc. When you've finished writing, review the list. Do any of those needs keep you stuck in a relationship that's not working or prevent you from having the conversation with your partner that would improve your current relationship? If so, can any of those needs be met within yourself?

Review your list again. Feeling whole or normal and feeling connected instead of lonely are inside jobs, our own personal responsibility. Other people can help, but if we don't feel connected on the inside with ourselves, then connection with others can be problematic. If we can meet our own needs, then our vision is clearer. We are free to see our partner for who they are. We are also free to love them for who they are, not who we need them to be.

The Third and Fourth Practices: Trust and Openness, Growing from Adversity

Facing our own needs is the work of the third and fourth practices. Let's go back to Dave and Mike, and Linda and Andrew, and look at how they worked these practices.

Dave had spent countless hours listening to Mike's troubles and fears. He tried to cheer Mike up, soothe his anxieties, and cocoon him from the world. Some people call this love. In the world of addiction treatment and codependence, it's called enabling. Without Dave's support, his listening ear, Mike might have been forced to manage his own anxieties. He might have found professional help. Or Mike might have walked away from the relationship, as he occasionally threatened to do. That was the risk Dave couldn't take until the pain of codependence forced him to get help.

The pain of extreme codependence is excruciating—every bit as excruciating as Mike's chronic anxiety. When Dave did take action and moved out of the apartment they shared, long, lonely evenings and endless weekends stretched ahead. Then a frightening thing happened: Dave's own demons began to surface. Dave could sink under his loneliness or he could explore his own painful past, particularly his relationship with his father. Dave bravely chose to trust the darkness and explore. In breathwork, Dave revisited memories of his father's coldness and the many public humiliations. He encountered fully the pain and loneliness of a child who felt completely worthless. He came out the other side deeply connected to himself. Had Mike also embraced awareness, the relationship might have survived, even thrived. But he didn't. While Dave deeply regretted that his relationship with Mike did not work out, he never regretted the process of spiritual growth that it forced him to embrace. Several years later, Dave sent me an e-mail. He wanted to tell me that he had found a new, less intense but far happier relationship.

Linda's need to be married stemmed in large part from her teenage years. A little overweight and a little less glamorous than her friends, she desperately wanted to fit in, to be "normal." For Linda's generation, normal meant married. She looked on as her friends and classmates found partners and started families. Linda was interested in her career, but she also wanted to be what she called a "normal woman." The more that eluded her, the deeper and more painful her craving for normalcy became. Then she met Andrew, and her career faded into the background.

Like Dave, Linda revisited the pain of her lonely teens, the anguish of feeling "like a freak," as she put it. And she too came out the other side. She came out of her dark night feeling "normal," not because she was now a married woman with a family just like her classmates, but because in breathwork she had reached a deep level of self-acceptance.

Several sessions into her therapy, Linda decided to speak to Andrew about what she called their "contract." Andrew couldn't understand what she was talking about, then got uncharacteristically furious at the whole idea that he might want to overshadow his wife. Linda weighed her options. She and Andrew were happy together. If she forced the issue with him, it could, she feared, end badly. But by that point, Linda had experienced connection with her Big Self. She trusted, a little shakily at times, that all would be well. She gave her husband time to cool down and prepared what she wanted to say to him.

Linda was remarkably responsible. She accepted that her stagnant career was the result of a choice she had made over twenty years earlier. So when she reopened the conversation with Andrew, she did so without blame or accusation. He responded more calmly this time, and over the next year they worked together to free Linda from her role of cheerleader. I can't say Linda's career took off from that point, because it didn't. But her real desire was to feel "normal," her code word for self-acceptance. Andrew remained the star, but self-acceptance and freedom from the burden of cheerleading changed the way Linda engaged with life. Ordinary life became richer for her, and in the process, the dream of a glittering, high-profile career lost its lure.

EXERCISE 41: HAVING THE CONVERSATION

Review your list of relationship needs from the previous exercise (exercise 40). Use your favorite exercise or technique from chapter 6 to help you meet the needs you have identified. This is deep work. You may have to revisit the process many times, and you may need the support of friends or a therapist/breathworker. Take as much time as you need.

When you've gotten a handle on meeting your own needs, take a look at your relationship. Is it safe to have some difficult conversations with your partner? If it is, make a list of what you would like from the relationship. Be sure to avoid blame. Here are some examples:

I would like us to share the housework and the care of the children as much as possible.	**NOT:** *You never do any of the housework and you never take care of the kids when I want to go out with my friends.*
I find being involved with the children very enjoyable. I'd love it if you could share that enjoyment and if you would give it a try. I'd like it if you'd join us when we play soccer together on Sunday.	**NOT:** *Why do you never play with the kids or help them with their homework?*
I'd like us to go out together on a "date" once a month.	**NOT:** *You never want to go anywhere.*

When you've completed your list, pick one or two of the least challenging items and find a good time to open the conversation with your partner. Don't expect instant results and don't be put off by initial negative responses. Your partner may not have dealt with his or her needs and fears as extensively as you have, so you may have to approach the conversation several times in different ways. If you're both willing to work together, couples therapy can be helpful.

I've spent many years working with people trapped in jealous or even abusive relationships. Sometimes the eventual and only solution is to do as Dave did and leave. But it's not the solution for everyone. If both parties are willing to embrace radical awareness, damaging and restrictive relationships can be transformed into something lifegiving and rewarding for both partners. Whether we choose to leave a relationship or work within it, we need both a strong Inner Witness and a level of spiritual trust that will see us through the difficult times. But the most valuable practice of all is the experience of oneness.

The Fifth Practice: Getting to One: Being awake going into a relationship may mean we're less driven to couple up. When we do get into a relationship that is not working well, that awful fear of loss is less likely to tie us to a lifetime of half-living. Our contemplative mind gives us the courage to face what's not working and transform it into something mutually nurturing, or to stop dancing. We have that courage partly because we trust the growth that comes from weathering the dark times if the relationship ends, painful as that may be. But we also have that courage because we have tasted the love that is at the heart of the experience of oneness.

When we have tasted oneness, we know that love has many sources: friends, parents, children, other family members, nature, pets, etc. But we also know that mystical love has no source but life itself. Mystical love is the air we breathe and the life we live. Mystical love is who we are, and it does not depend on any one type of relationship.

We began this chapter with medieval poets. Here is twentieth-century poet and mystic Kahlil Gibran writing about marriage:

> *Love one another, but make not a bond of love...*
> *Fill each other's cup, but drink not from one cup...*
> *Give your hearts, but not into each other's keeping.*
> *For only the hand of Life can contain your hearts.* [44]

Our culture's definition of romantic love is replete with images of hearts given away, of the handing over of self to another, of happiness created by, and therefore dependent on, our lover. Gibran's beautiful description of marriage is the antithesis of this. When the hand of life, rather than our partner, holds our heart, we are freed from the emotional dependency that can sour potentially good relationships. As Anthony de Mello describes it, "it is... a kind of symphony, a kind of orchestra that plays one melody in your presence, but when you depart, the orchestra doesn't stop. When I meet someone else, it plays another melody, which is also very delightful. And when I'm alone, it continues to play. There's a great repertoire and it never ceases to play." [45] The orchestra may play a different melody for each source of love, but the greatest love is within us. This is where all the awareness, all the trust, the rough road of self-examination, all the exercises, the breathwork, and meditation, lead—to oneness and the all-encompassing, all-embracing love we find there. It's a love that liberates us from need and, in doing so, empowers us to experience the kind of romantic love that nurtures rather than restricts.

EXERCISE 42: EXPERIENCING ONENESS

The most reliable way to experience the mystical love that is at the heart of oneness is through a consistently practiced spiritual technique. Choose the technique from chapter 6 that you find most effective, then practice it regularly. If your chosen technique is meditation or a breathwork exercise, practice daily for at least one month. If you choose a yoga class, accelerated breathwork, or a form of therapy, the intervals between sessions will be longer but must still be consistent. You might like to keep a journal of your experiences, but the most important thing is to set aside as much time as you need to practice regularly.

14
LETTING GO WITH EASE

When one door of happiness closes, another opens; but often we look so long at the closed door that we do not see the one which has been opened for us.

~HELEN KELLER

My stomach heaved viciously. I doubled over, clutching my middle. The cramps had wrenched me out of sleep, then kept on coming, wave after wave of contractions. I'd had enough food poisoning in my travels to recognize the symptoms, but this was the worst I'd ever experienced. I glanced at the digital clock glowing red through the darkness: 3:00 a.m. My hostess was asleep in the next room. I didn't want to wake her, but I needed a toilet. I needed it right away!

I stumbled out of bed and groped my way through the tiny house. My stomach heaved again. The darkness shifted and pleated. I held tighter to the wall, the bare concrete floor rough and cool beneath my feet. Then I found the bathroom and flipped the light switch, grateful to have been housed in a home that actually had a bathroom. The tiny cubicle glowed sepia in the dull light. But as I leaned over the toilet, everything went black.

I was a guest in one of the homes that, in a fit of planning madness, had been constructed on the former city dump in Juarez, Mexico. My visit was part of a group retreat organized by the Center for Action and Contemplation in Albuquerque, New Mexico. A few days living in poverty in the stomping ground of the drug cartels was meant to deepen our awareness of social justice. It did a lot more than that for me.

I came to on my back, my head wedged into the small space between the toilet bowl and the wall. I stared up at the circle of yellowed light on the cracked ceiling. Although the house had indoor plumbing, the system wasn't robust enough to handle paper, so the odor from the can of used toilet roll washed over me. I lay on the floor not able to move, my mind a complete blank—until a thought struck, a thought as powerful as the cramp that had catapulted me from sleep.

My hostess and I were about the same age. In a few days I would return to my spacious, beautiful home in Dublin, my fully functioning bathroom, and my well-paying, secure job. But the generous, kind woman who was sharing her home and meager food supply with me had to live in these conditions for the rest of her life. No reprieve. No way out. That realization of the contrast between us knocked something loose inside me. I didn't know what it was at the time, but I could feel it shift.

I had arrived in Albuquerque looking to change my life. I wasn't too clear about the specifics of how that would happen, or that it would happen at all, but I was banking on it. The previous few years had brought an onslaught of loss and bereavement, including the death of my parents. My life had dried up on the inside, had lost all its meaning and juice. But I clung to the outside—to my job, to security, to my home. Arid and meaningless as my life had become, I couldn't let it go. And if I couldn't let go, I couldn't move on to something more fulfilling. That night in Juarez, I let go of my old life. I didn't realize until much later that letting go doesn't have to be such a struggle.

Stuff Happens

I grew up listening to phrases like "Out with the old, in with the new" and "When one door closes, another door opens." At the time, these sayings seemed like clichéd nonsense that old people trotted out when they couldn't think of anything useful to say. If I'd had enough sense to pay attention back then, I probably wouldn't have ended up passed out in a bathroom five thousand miles from home. Those simple old phrases would have told me everything I needed to know about letting go.

The old sayings tell us, first of all, that life is a constant movement toward change. No matter how hard we fight against it, the flow of change never ceases. Some changes are thrust upon us. A partner decides to end our relationship, we lose our job, or someone we love dies. Sometimes we are the ones who initiate the change. We change careers, we end relationships, we return to school. Whether we initiate change or have it foisted upon us, the flow goes on, with or without our permission.

This constant movement can be painful, but when we try to prevent change from taking place, life becomes a dried-up shell. The shell may be beautiful, packed with familiar shapes and forms, but devoid of the spiritual vitality that animates our existence. If we are to grow spiritually, we need to learn to embrace change. And the essential skill required to change is the ability to let go. Letting go allows us to flow with life. We cannot plan or strive or force ourselves into oneness; we can only let go into it.

Letting go can be so natural and easy, we barely notice it. When daylight begins to fade, we let go of the expectation of light and move into darkness. We may desire a few more hours of daylight, but we know that night is inevitable. And because we know night is inevitable, we stop doing the things we do in daylight and move on to the things we do indoors. The next morning, daylight returns and the endless cycle continues. Moving from day to night is a daily experience of letting go, and we all have the ability to do it.

Like the movement from day to night, when one door closes, another opens, and we simply walk on through. But sometimes we cling so tightly to what lies behind that closed door that we don't even notice the new door opening behind us. At times like this, letting go can feel like such a monumental struggle that we long for something or someone to kick us through the change and into our future. Therapists often call this "being stuck."

I had reached that point before traveling to Juarez. My stuckness made that letting-go experience seem dramatic and out of the blue. In reality, I had simply reached the endpoint of a lot of inner work. There are several stages to the inner work that lead us to the point of letting go: facing the reality of our situation, mourning our loss, and building the foundation for our future. For those of us who struggle with the process of letting go, the contemplative mind—the product of working the five practices—can teach us how to flow through each of these stages with greater ease and grace. We can plot out the process through the experience of my client Oliver.

Awareness and Letting Go: The Gift of Reality

Forced Change: Oliver's girlfriend left him after three years. They had shared an apartment for two of those years and had talked openly about a future together. Then one day, she told him she needed space. That evening she moved out. Oliver reeled from the punch of her move. He had contemplated asking his girlfriend to marry him and had even looked at some engagement rings. Her departure left a giant hole in his future.

Oliver then did what many people do when change has been forced upon them against their will: he analyzed. What had gone wrong? What had he done wrong? If he had done this or that differently, would the relationship have worked? If she loved him as much as she said she did, how could she leave him? He needed an explanation, but his ex-girlfriend gave him a cliché. Every time he called, she told him the same thing—she needed space. This information vacuum allowed Oliver to hope there was a chance of winning her back, something he fantasized about daily.

The reason we analyze obsessively when change is forced upon us is because we scramble to make sense of what has just occurred. And maybe, we think, just maybe, if we really understand, we can reverse the change. But, as in Oliver's case, we may never fully understand what happened. Why does a child die, for example? Why does the world economy crash and we lose our job when others hold on to theirs? Why does someone who tells us they love us suddenly leave? Some questions have no answers. All we can do is recognize that whatever has happened has happened. The situation we find ourselves in is reality. Our reality.

Reality can be hard to accept. We can seek refuge from it in blame. Oliver swung between blaming himself for what happened and blaming his ex-girlfriend. In between, he criticized himself for not being able to move on. Analysis and blame served a purpose. They always do. They buffered Oliver against the immediate, possibly overwhelming implications of his loss. Like many of us, Oliver needed to face his reality in increments.

I remember Oliver's first session as being a deluge of stories, what ifs, and whys. During his second session, I asked him to take a few deep breaths into his belly. The technique worked. Deep breathing calmed the storm of words for moments at a time. With practice, the periods of stillness grew longer, and Oliver discovered that he could rest in the stillness of the present moment while his world roiled around him. By pulling us into the present moment, meditation and breathwork can act like mini-vacations. And like vacations, they give us time to gather our resources and face our troubles refreshed.

Gradually, Oliver learned to work the second practice (Living in the Present) skillfully. He learned to trust the fact that in the midst of his pain, he could be at peace. As peace seeped out from the breathwork sessions into Oliver's daily life, the pain of his loss retreated. What had felt like a knife in his guts became a dull ache. With the foundation of trust well established, Oliver's Inner Witness brought him face to face with the fact that his girlfriend was gone and she was not coming back. He didn't stop wanting her back, but he accepted that it was never going to happen. And he discovered that much of the pain we experience in letting go is related to our resistance to facing our reality, to acknowledging that the door is indeed closed. For Oliver, finally accepting reality brought an unexpected and welcome sense of relief.

Self-Initiated Change: When change is self-initiated, the process often begins with a sense of dissatisfaction, a malaise. Initially, the cause of this malaise is not always apparent. But as dissatisfaction grows, the picture becomes clearer. We may have outgrown some aspect of our life—our job, for example. Work that was once stimulating is now boring, but the pay is good, the benefits are exceptional, and we can walk to work. Changing jobs is hard work, and who knows, we might hate the new job once we got it. We can analyze and agonize over self-initiated change in much the same way Oliver did over forced change. We can hang on for as long as possible to a dying relationship or a job that's no longer challenging. At some point, like Oliver, we have to face what is, right now. We have to face the fact that what once engaged, stimulated, and animated us is gone. We have grown out of the skin of our life.

But discernment is not always easy or clear-cut. If some part of our life—a relationship, a job, etc.—feels stagnant, or something we want is just not happening, no matter how badly we want it or how hard we work at it, that door may have closed for us. But how can we tell whether it's really a closed door or just something that requires a little more time, patience, and effort on our part? If you're not too sure about change and movement in your life right now, the following exercise can help you reach a deeper level of clarity.

EXERCISE 43: IS THE DOOR REALLY CLOSED?

You'll need a pen, some paper, and a space to be alone. Choose an aspect of your life right now where you feel stuck. Ground yourself with your favorite breathing or meditation exercise from chapter 6, then begin writing. Sample answers have been included with each instruction.

1. Describe the situation briefly.

   a) My boyfriend doesn't contact me, sometimes for over a week at a time.

   b) My job is boring.

2. How long has the situation persisted?

   a) Eighteen months.

   b) About a year.

3. Was it always that way?

   a) Yes, we've been together for eighteen months.

   b) No. For the first five years it was interesting.

4. What have you done to rectify the situation?

   a) I talked to him, I pleaded with him, told him I'd leave. We went to counseling.

   b) I try to see the value in what I do. I think about my paycheck. I plan my weekend during work.

5. Is there anything else you could do?

   a) I've tried everything except actually leaving.

   b) I could talk to my manager about new projects or about moving to a new department.

6. Take twenty connected breaths and give a quick, spontaneous gut answer to the following question: If it hasn't worked out by now, will it ever work?

   a) No.

   b) It might if I come up with a plan and talk to my manager.

In the first example, if the boyfriend hasn't responded by now, he's unlikely to change his behavior in the future. This is probably a closed door. His girlfriend now has the choice to end the relationship or to accept her boyfriend as he is. In the second example, the door may also be closed, but it's too early to tell because the work of taking responsibility for improving the situation has not yet been done.

This exercise is one tool you can use to help with discernment. It should only be used in combination with other methods of decision making that work for you—meditation, prayer, talking things over with friends, family, or a counselor, or whatever has helped you in the past. If, after a thorough process of discernment, you think the door has been closed, take all the time you need to figure out what, if any, action you wish to take. Letting go can lead to a big, visible, dramatic change, but most of the time, changes are smaller, more gradual, and often not visible at all. And sometimes, what we need to let go of is limited ways of thinking (attitudes and beliefs) that no longer serve us well.

GROWING FROM ADVERSITY:
THE SKILL OF MOURNING WELL

Most of us would prefer not to have to face a closed door, but often, as with Oliver, accepting reality brings a tremendous flood of relief. That is because we've become unstuck. We're in motion once more. But what we're leaving behind is important. For better or worse, it made us who we now are. To move on effectively, we need to mourn our loss. Mourning can be painful, but it's a good kind of pain, the kind of pain that tells us we have rejoined the flow of life. If we linger too long in mourning, it can turn to depression. But if we don't mourn, we run the risk of not being able to let go completely.

During the time leading up to acceptance, Oliver reviewed the three years of his relationship. But that review took place amid the frenzy of analysis and blame. During mourning, Oliver continued to review, but calmly this time, in the light of acceptance. He examined what was good about his relationship—the vacation he and his girl-friend had taken together in Thailand, how he loved the way her skin glowed after a shower, how she listened so intently to the details of his day at work.

Oliver's mourning found expression in gestures and ritual. Throughout history, people have used ritual to mark and move through the most important experiences and transitions of life. For each aspect of the relationship, Oliver created his own ritual. He stared at photos of himself and his ex-girlfriend together. He wrote letters to her that he would never send. He gave away the things she had left in their apartment. But he carried out these actions mindfully, with total awareness of the sorrow and the farewell inherent in each gesture, each ritual. Oliver was saying goodbye to what was and to what might have been.

There are other ways to mourn—crying, periods of solitude, re-visiting significant locations from the past, etc. When someone we love dies, the funeral can be therapeutic. At funerals, we get to share memories of the person who has died. We don't just say farewell, we celebrate their life. It's common to feel anger toward someone who has ended a relationship against our will. But we can also be angry at someone we love for dying, particularly if they chose to die by suicide. Where anger is an element, mourning can include punching pillows, shouting, and screaming.

Mourning is not always about bereavement or desertion. Particularly in cases of abuse, we mourn the life we never had, the life we feel has been stolen from us by abuse. We mourn the loss of aspects of ourselves. That particular type of loss runs deep.

These times of mourning can be dark and difficult. But the fourth practice, Growing from Adversity, can sustain us through the darkest of times. Along the path of mourning, we brush up against the love and security inherent in the state of oneness. We reconnect with our Big Self. There is no more secure, warm, and comforting place to rest than in our Big Self. In deep connection with our true self, there is no past or future, only the present. In the eternal present, emotions lose their sting. That makes mourning more manageable. The experience of reconnecting with our Big Self assures us that we can trust the darkness, that there is a new door opening even if we can't yet see it.

EXERCISE 44: RITUAL MOURNING

If you're in the process of mourning a loss, it can help to create rituals for yourself. For example:

• Make a collection of items that remind you of the person or situation you're letting go of. Then slowly, with full awareness, feed those items into a fire, or bury them. Some people like to plant a flower over the spot where they've buried their chosen items. You can do this kind of ritual alone or with friends as witnesses.

- If you find writing or journaling useful, it can help to write a letter to the person, the organization, even the situation you want to leave behind. This kind of letter is designed to be ritually burned or torn up, not mailed to the person in question.

- Some people like to go out alone into nature to a place where they can be completely alone, to create symbols from plants and stone or to say goodbye aloud. This can be painful, but is ultimately liberating.

Foundations Built on Oneness

Oliver arrived for his therapy session looking a little shaken. He had spent the previous night with his older sister, Liz, and her family. Liz worked as an IT consultant, and over dinner, the topic of Facebook came up in conversation. Oliver mentioned that he had recently unfriended his ex-girlfriend.

"You unfriended her?" Liz asked. "Not the other way around?"

"I unfriended her," Oliver said. "What's so odd about that?"

"The fact that you did it," she answered. "You never do stuff like that."

"What stuff?" Oliver asked, mildly offended.

"Stand-up-for-yourself stuff." Liz put down her fork and glared at her brother. "Do you have any idea how annoying that gets, you agreeing with things all the time?"

Liz later apologized for being so sharp with her brother, but what she said got Oliver thinking. What role had he played in the breakdown of his relationship?

Oliver had indeed been passive with his ex-girlfriend. He had been so afraid of losing her, of losing anyone in his life, that he kept silent even when she told him about the men at work who wanted to date her. She had played on his insecurity. But Oliver had a lot of insecurity to be played upon. And that problem was Oliver's alone to deal with.

The process of letting go prepares us for whatever comes next. As part of letting go, we must lay the foundation on which that future will be built. We played a role in shaping the life, the relationship, or the job that we're now leaving behind. If we don't examine that role, we may find that our future comes to resemble our past.

Oliver believed he needed to be with one special someone in order to be happy. Like Dave in the previous chapter, the prospect of life alone frightened Oliver. This made him needy, and neediness turned him into a passive partner. In many ways, Oliver hadn't been present in his relationship. If Oliver didn't address this issue, his next relationship could well end the same way.

The bliss of oneness that comes at the end of a breathwork session was key to resolving Oliver's insecurity. In the mystical experience of oneness, there is no emotional need. When there is no emotional need, there is no insecurity. The experience of being held and nurtured by life during mystical states began to permeate the rest of Oliver's life. His insecurity faded to the point where he began to enjoy his own company. For him, a future alone was not ideal, but the prospect of living alone for the rest of his life ceased to terrify him. That gaping hole had closed up without him even noticing it shrinking. In opening to the state of oneness, Oliver built the foundation for his future relationships.

EXERCISE 45: SOLID FOUNDATIONS

If you have worked your way through this book using the exercises in each chapter, you are probably keenly aware of what you have brought to the situation you described in Exercise 43: Is the Door Really Closed? The next step is to clarify exactly what you need to move forward. You will need a pen and notebook. Use your favorite breathing exercise from chapter 6. When you're centered and fully present in the now, complete this starter sentence: "To build a solid foundation for moving on, I need to ..."

Here are some sample answers to get you thinking:

"To build a solid foundation for moving on, ..."

- I need to take college courses.
- I need to value myself more.
- I need to be more assertive.
- I need to say what I need in the relationship early on.
- I need to stop caring so much about what people think of me—to approve of myself.
- I need to meditate regularly.

The responses will be unique to each person and each situation. Some foundation-building activities may be concrete and practical—saving money or taking a college course, for example. Some may be more nebulous—fulfilling our own needs or finding self-acceptance, for example. But foundation building ensures that when we step through that newly opened door, our future will not be a repetition of our past.

Letting Go

The stages of letting go—accepting reality, mourning, and foundation building—do not progress in sequence, nor are they separate and discrete activities. All three aspects of the work of letting go run together, weaving in and out of each other. There's no time frame. For each person, letting go takes as long as it takes, but the process can be speeded up through engagement with a spiritual technique or therapy. The reward of letting go can't be determined or planned ahead of time, but the contemplative mind and the old clichés tell us there will be a reward. That new door will open.

Life is a constant process of growth and transition. Even death can be seen as a transition into a new, as yet undefined, phase of existence. In every phase of life, we face obstacles that spur us on, that challenge us to become our truest self. The elements of letting go prepare us for what comes next. The challenges of the past have been met. We are ready to take on the new challenges, the new opportunities for growth that lie just ahead. Letting go is what allows the new door to open and empowers us to walk through it.

Oliver let go of his old relationship, his insecurity, and his dream of the future. In Juarez, I let go of a life. I felt sure there would be another relationship for Oliver, but if not, he would go into his future with himself as his partner. That assurance was the door that opened for him. Within a year of my experience in Mexico, I had moved to another country, started a completely new job, and found the inspiration for a new book. These were the doors that opened for me. The reward of letting go is not just freedom from the struggle created by our attachment to what once was or what will never be. Letting go opens the way for new life, for new adventures, for gritty engagement with what is. Letting go frees us to storm our own version of heaven.

EXERCISE 46: LETTING GO

One of the best techniques for letting go is a full, dynamic breathwork session. This should be done with a trained therapist. If you don't have a therapist, the following exercise can help, particularly if you repeat it daily.

Use the twenty connected breaths (exercise 12) from chapter 6 to establish your breathing pattern, then ease down the volume of your inhale. When you have a comfortable rhythm, hold whatever you want to let go of in your awareness. It can help some people to visualize it as an object, a symbol, a color. For others, holding it in awareness is sufficient. Then see it slowly drifting away from you. Let it drift until it's out of sight. You may have an emotional reaction to this—sadness, for example. Just keep breathing until it passes.

CONCLUSION

When we want to get from point A to point B, we plan our journey. We've learned, for example, that the number 46 bus will pick us up at point A and take us to point B, so we wait at the point A bus stop, hop on the 46 when it arrives, and are certain it will take us to point B.

In the world of spiritual development, the only thing we know for certain is that we should wait at the point A bus stop and, while we're waiting, keep our mind and eyes open. The transportation will arrive, but it may not be the number 46. It may not even be a bus. And while it could indeed leave us at point B, it could just as easily leave us at point C, D, or E. There is no way to know where spiritual growth will lead until we get there. And even when we arrive, the place we arrive at is just a stopping point on the way to somewhere else. The joy is in the journey, wherever it takes us.

This book gives us a tool kit for opening our mind, our eyes, and our heart to the infinite possibilities life offers. When life is difficult and painful, when it seems as if nothing is happening and nothing ever will, we are, in reality, right in the middle of the most fertile time for spiritual growth. We may not be able to see it at the time, but we are on the threshold of opportunity. The opportunity will come. Our job is to be patient and to develop our awareness to the point where we recognize the opportunity when it arrives. The five practices—radical awareness, the ability to live in the present moment, the ability to trust and stay open to life through the darkest of times, and the experience of being one with life—these are the tools that prepare us. These are the means by which we develop a contemplative mind.

Because the contemplative mind engages with every moment, life becomes rich. That richness is enough. It's all we need. But the spiritual paradox is that when we are engaged with life, when we are filled and satisfied by the present, that is when life presents opportunities for adventure. And on those adventures, the five practices help us engage deeply and profit greatly from anything life brings our way.

The contemplative mind is not a formula for worldly success. It does not map out a path to getting what we think we want in life. Instead, the contemplative mind gives us the keys to living our lives abundantly. It gives us a level of peace and freedom that will stand up to the pressures of life so that we can engage with that life, whatever shape it takes, fully and completely. The aliveness, the happiness, we crave lies in our engagement with life, not in our ability to get to point B. But when we are alive and awake, the limitations we have set for ourselves dissolve. Point B, once the focus of our dreams and longings, may lose its luster and seem limited and circumscribed. This is because we now have a much wider world to explore. And, in the five practices, we have the ability, the trust, and the courage to go out and explore it.

This book is a starter guide to spiritual exploration. It is a "finger pointing to the moon." From here on, the exploration is experiential—the theory must be put into practice. This means choosing and using your own method for working the five practices, for getting to oneness. Please use the exercises sprinkled throughout this book to help you become a fully engaged traveler. Find the support you need from friends, family, a therapist, or a teacher. But above all, trust that the view from point C, D, or E can be just as spectacular as the view from point B. Life has amazing adventures in store for us just as soon as we are ready to enjoy the journey.

Recommended Reading

General

Beattie, Melody. *Codependent No More*. Hazelden, 1987.

Brazier, David. *Zen Therapy*. Constable & Robinson Ltd., 1995.

Bronkhorst, Johannes. *Absorption*. UniversityMedia, 2012.

Chödrön, Pema. *When Things Fall Apart*. Shambhala, 1997.

De Mello, Anthony. *Awareness*. Fount Paperbacks, 1990.

Dyer, Wayne W. *What Do You Really Want for Your Children?* Avon, 1985.

Ellis, Albert. *Humanistic Psychotherapy*. Julian Press, 1973.

Erikson, Erik. *Childhood and Society*. Penguin, 1965.

Frankl, Viktor. *Man's Search for Meaning*. Washington Square Press, 1959.

Gibran, Kahlil. *The Prophet*. Alfred A. Knopf, 1979.

Goleman, Daniel. *Emotional Intelligence*. Bloomsbury, 1996.

Habecker, Kelsea. *Hollow Out*. New Rivers Press, 2008.

Hay, Louise. *You Can Heal Your Life*. Eden Grove, 1988.

Humphreys, Tony. *Myself, My Partner.* Gill & Macmillan, 1998.

Jung, C. G. *Memories, Dreams, Reflections.* A. Jaffe, ed. Fontana, 1995.

Maslow, Abraham. *Religions, Values and Peak Experiences.* Penguin, 1964.

McFetridge, Grant. *Peak States of Consciousness: Theory and Applications, Volumes 1 & 2.* Institute for the Study of Peak States, 2004.

Moore, Thomas. *Care of the Soul: A Guide for Cultivating Depth and Sacredness in Everyday Life.* HarperPerennial, 1994.

———. *Dark Nights of the Soul: A Guide to Finding Your Way Through Life's Ordeals.* Gotham, 2004.

Obama, Barack. *The Audacity of Hope.* Canongate, 2007.

O'Leary, Daniel. *Travelling Light: Your Journey to Wholeness.* Columba, 2005.

Patel, Chandra. *The Complete Guide to Stress Management.* Optima, 1989.

Peck, M. Scott. *The Road Less Traveled.* Rider, 1997.

Ray, Sondra, and Bob Mandel. *Birth and Relationships: How Your Birth Affects Your Relationships.* Celestial Arts, 1987.

Riso, Don Richard, and Russ Hudson. *The Wisdom of the Enneagram: The Complete Guide to Psychological and Spiritual Growth for the Nine Personality Types.* Bantam, 1999.

Rohr, Richard. *Everything Belongs: The Gift of Contemplative Prayer.* Crossroads, 2003.

Rosenberg, Jack Lee, with Marjorie L. Rand and Diane Asay. *Body, Self and Soul: Sustaining Integration.* Humanics Ltd., 1991.

Saunders, Alex, with Carole Epstein, Gill Keep, and Thangam Debbonaire. *It Hurts Me Too: Children's Experiences of Domestic Violence.* Saunders, WAFF, NISW, Childline, 1995.

Stevens, Jay. *Storming Heaven: LSD and the American Dream.* Paladin, 1987.

Stone, Hal, and Sidra Stone. *Embracing Our Selves: The Voice Dialogue Manual.* New World Library, 1989.

Walsh, Roger, and Frances Vaughan. *Paths Beyond Ego: The Transpersonal Vision.* Penguin Putnam, 1993.

Watts, Alan. *The Book: On the Taboo Against Knowing Who You Are.* Vintage, 1966.

Whitfield, M.D., Charles L. *Co-Dependence: Healing the Human Condition.* Health Communications, 1991.

Wilber, Ken. *A Brief History of Everything.* Shambhala, 2000.

Yalom, Irvin D. *The Theory and Practice of Group Psychotherapy.* Basic Books, 1975.

Breathwork/Meditation

Begg, Deike. *Rebirthing: Freedom from Your Past.* Thorsons, 1999.

Dowling, Catherine. *Rebirthing and Breathwork: A Powerful Technique for Personal Transformation.* Piatkus, 2000.

Fried, Robert. *Breathe Well, Be Well.* John Wiley & Sons, 1999.

Grof, Stanislav, and Christina Grof. *The Stormy Search for the Self.* Thorsons, 1995.

Hendricks, Gay. *Conscious Breathing: Breathwork for Health, Stress Release, and Personal Mastery.* Bantam, 1995.

Manné, Joy. *Conscious Breathing: How Shamanic Breathwork Can Transform Your Life.* North Atlantic Books, 2004.

———. *Soul Therapy.* North Atlantic Books, 1997.

Manné, Joy, ed. *The Healing Breath: A Journal of Breathwork Practice, Psychology and Spirituality.* www.healingbreathjournal.org. Also available with kind permission from Dr. Joy Manné on my website, www.catherinedowling.com.

Minett, Gunnel. *Breath and Spirit: Rebirthing as a Healing Tool.* Aquarian Press, 1994.

Moore, Robert, ed. *Breathe: The International Breathwork Magazine.* 7 Silver Street, Buckfastleigh, Devon TQ11 OBQ, UK.

Ray, Sondra. *Celebration of Breath.* Celestial Arts, 1983.

Salzberg, Sharon, Sakyong Mipham, Tulku Thondup, and Larry Rosenberg. *Quiet Mind: A Beginner's Guide to Meditation.* Shambhala, 2002.

Saraswati, Swami Ambikananda. *Principles of Breathwork.* Thorsons, 1999.

Sissons, Colin. *Rebirthing Made Easy.* Total Press, 1985.

Taylor, Kylea. *The Breathwork Experience: Exploration and Healing in Nonordinary States of Consciousness.* Hanford Mead, 1994.

Notes

Introduction

1. George H. Gallup, Jr., "Religious Awakenings Bolster Americans' Faith," Gallup (January 14, 2003), www.gallup.com/poll/7582 /religious-awakenings-bolster-americans-faith.aspx.

2. "Results from the 2011 National Survey on Drug Use and Health: Mental Health Findings," US Department of Health and Human Services, www.samhsa.gov/data/NSDUH/2k11MH _FindingsandDetTables/2K11MHFR/NSDUHmhfr2011.htm.

Chapter 1

3. Grant McFetridge, *Oneness States of Consciousness: Theory and Applications, Volumes 1 & 2,* Institute for the Study of Peak States, 2004.

4. See "Ozymandias" by Percy Bysshe Shelley, for example.

5. Diane Zimberoff and David Hartman, "Breathwork: Exploring the Frontier of 'Being' and 'Doing,'" *Journal of Heart-Centered Therapies* vol. 2, no. 2 (1999), pp. 3–52, www.wellness-institute .org/images/Journal_2-2_Breath_Therapy.pdf.

6. Johannes Bronkhorst, *Absorption*, UniversityMedia (2012).

7. Ken Wilber, *A Brief History of Everything*, Shambhala (2000), p. 34.

Chapter 2

8. Pema Chödrön, *When Things Fall Apart*, Shambhala (1997), p. 10.

Chapter 3

9. This is a favorite phrase of Richard Rohr and is used throughout his writing.

10. Julian of Norwich, fourteenth-century English mystic, in her book *Revelations of Divine Love*.

11. Anthony de Mello, *Awareness*, Fount Paperbacks (1990).

Chapter 4

12. Laboratory of Neuro Imaging at the University of Southern California, http://www.loni.usc.edu/about_loni/education /brain_trivia.php.

13. Pema Chödrön, *When Things Fall Apart*, Shambhala (1997), p. 2.

14. Daniel O'Leary, *Travelling Light: Your Journey to Wholeness*, Columba (2005), p. 61.

15. Ibid., p. 145.

Chapter 5

16. Thomas Moore, *Care of the Soul: How to Add Depth and Meaning to Your Everyday Life*, Harper (1998), p. 112.

17. Pema Chödrön, *When Things Fall Apart*, Shambhala (1997), p. 13.

18. Richard Rohr, *Everything Belongs*, Crossroads (2003), p. 155.

19. Ibid.

20. Daniel O'Leary, *Travelling Light*, Columba (2005), p. 168.

21. Barack Obama, *The Audacity of Hope*, Canongate (2007), p. 33.

22. Joan Chittister, *Illuminated Life: Monastic Wisdom for Seekers of Light*, Orbis (2000), p. 129.

23. Etty Hillesum, *Etty Hillesum: An Interrupted Life and Letters from Westerbork*, Henry Holt (1996), p. 183.

24. Daniel O'Leary, *Travelling Light*, Columba (2005), p. 102.

25. Ken Wilber, *A Brief History of Everything*, Shambhala (2000), p. 208.

CHAPTER 6

26. Dr. D. R Johnson, "Introductory Anatomy: Respiratory System," Faculty of Biological Sciences, University of Leeds, www.leeds.ac.uk/chb/lectures/anatomy7.html.

27. John R. Holmes, PhD, "How Much Air Do We Breathe?," California Environmental Protection Agency Air Resources Board, Aug. 1994, www.arb.ca.gov/research/resnotcs/notes/94-11.htm.

28. Robert L. Fried, *Breathe Well, Be Well*, John Wiley & Sons (1999), p. 130.

29. Pierre Philippot, Gaëtane Chapelle, and Sylvie Blairy, "Respiratory Feedback in the Generation of Emotion," *Cognition and Emotion*, vol. 16, issue 5 (2002), www.tandfonline.com/doi/abs/10.1080/02699930143000392?journalCode=pcem20#.UhqLntLn91o.

30. Project Welcome Home Troops, Power Breath Workshop, www.projectwelcomehometroops.org/power-breath-workshop.

31. Norman A. S. Farb, Zindel V. Segal, and Adam K. Anderson, "Attentional Modulation of Primary Interoceptive and Exteroceptive Cortices," *Cerebral Cortex* (January 19, 2012), http://

cercor.oxfordjournals.org/content/early/2012/01/19/cercor.bhr 385.full.pdf+html.

32. Jon Kabat-Zinn, "Cultivating Mindfulness: Beginning or Deepening a Personal Meditation Practice," http://static.oprah.com/download/pdfs/presents/2007/spa/spa_meditate_cultivate.pdf.

CHAPTER 8

33. Richard Rohr, *Everything Belongs,* Crossroads (2003), p. 158.

34. Don Richard Riso and Russ Hudson, *The Wisdom of the Enneagram: The Complete Guide to Psychological and Spiritual Growth for the Nine Personality Types,* Bantam (1999).

35. Pres. Franklin D. Roosevelt, inaugural address, March 4, 1933.

CHAPTER 9

36. Mawlana Jalal ad-Din Rumi, "There Is a Field."

CHAPTER 12

37. Pema Chödrön, *When Things Fall Apart,* Shambhala (1997), p. 103.

CHAPTER 13

38. Andreas Capellanus, *De Amore (On Love: A Treatise on Courtly Love).*

39. "Courtly love" is a term that came into use in the nineteenth century to describe the literary genre popular in medieval Europe, particularly France.

40. Anthony de Mello, *Awareness,* Fount Paperbacks (1990), p. 40.

41. Ibid., p. 118.

42. Ayn Rand, *For the New Intellectual*, Random House (1961), p. 118.

43. Anthony de Mello, *Awareness*, Fount Paperbacks (1990), p. 118.

44. Kahlil Gibran, *The Prophet*, "On Marriage," Alfred A. Knopf (1979), pp. 15–16.

45. Anthony de Mello, *Awareness*, Fount Paperbacks (1990), p. 54.

USEFUL CONTACTS

Association for Humanistic Psychology: www.ahpweb.org

Australian Breathwork Association: www.australianbreathwork association.org.au

Breathing Circle: www.breathingcircle.com

British Rebirth Society (UK): www.rebirthingbreathwork.co.uk

Catherine Dowling: www.catherinedowling.com/blog

Center for Compassion and Altruism Research and Education: ccare.stanford.edu

Enneagram Institute: www.enneagraminstitute.com

Gestalt Therapy Page: www.gestalt.org

Global Professional Breathwork Alliance: www.breathworkalliance .com

Grof: www.holotropic.com

Institute for the Study of Peak States: www.peakstates.com

International Breathwork Foundation: www.ibfnetwork.org

International Family Therapy Association: www.ifta-familytherapy
  .org

Transformations, Inc. (USA): www.transformationsusa.com

ACKNOWLEDGMENTS

With gratitude to Lar, Olivia, Lucy, Kelsea, Noor, Joy, and Patty for your unwavering support and uncompromising critiques. You all played a vital role. Thank you to Charlotte and to the members of Our Voices writing group—Dave, Maddy, Linda, and Richard—for ensuring I faced the empty page, and to the staff of the Center for Action and Contemplation, particularly Vanessa, Anita, Mary Jo, and Erica, for experiences beyond the ordinary. Thanks too to my friends in the breathwork community around the world, and lastly, to Angela Wix of Llewellyn Worldwide for recognizing and shepherding this project from concept to book.

To Write to the Author

If you wish to contact the author or would like more information about this book, please write to the author in care of Llewellyn Worldwide Ltd. and we will forward your request. Both the author and publisher appreciate hearing from you and learning of your enjoyment of this book and how it has helped you. Llewellyn Worldwide Ltd. cannot guarantee that every letter written to the author can be answered, but all will be forwarded. Please write to:

Catherine Dowling
⅝ Llewellyn Worldwide
2143 Wooddale Drive
Woodbury, MN 55125-2989
Please enclose a self-addressed stamped envelope for reply,
or $1.00 to cover costs. If outside the U.S.A., enclose
an international postal reply coupon.

Many of Llewellyn's authors have websites with additional information and resources. For more information, please visit our website at http://www.llewellyn.com.